THE ASSIGNMENT:

THE PAIN
&
THE PASSION

MIKE MURDOCK

Unless otherwise indicated, all Scripture quotations are taken from the King James Version of the Bible.

The Assignment: The Pain & The Passion, Volume 4
ISBN 1-56394-056-6
Copyright ©1999 by Mike Murdock

Published by
Wisdom International
P.O. Box 99
Denton, Texas 76202

Printed in the United States of America.

Contents

1

THE PROBLEM GOD CREATED YOU TO SOLVE ON EARTH IS YOUR ASSIGNMENT.

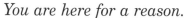

You are here for a reason.

To assign means to set apart or mark for a specific purpose. "But know that the Lord hath set apart him that is godly for himself" (Psalm 4:3).

The Bible, The Manufacturer's Handbook, is filled with examples of those who discovered and embraced their Assignment.

▶ *Moses* solved problems for the *Israelites*.
▶ *Aaron* solved problems for *Moses*.
▶ *Jonathan* was assigned to *David*.
▶ *Jonah* was assigned to the *Ninevites*.
▶ A *handmaiden* helped *Naaman* get healed.
▶ *Ruth* was assigned to *Naomi*.

You, too, are assigned to solve problems.

For somebody.

Somewhere.

You are the *Healer* for someone sick.

You are the *Life-jacket* for someone drowning.

You are the *Ruler* over someone unruly.

You are the *Lifter* for someone fallen.

You have asked these questions a thousand times. *Why* am I here? Why *me*? What is my *purpose*? Is there *really* a God? Where did I come from? Did I exist in another world before this one?

A poem is the proof of a *poet.*

A song is the proof of a *composer.*

A product is the proof of a *manufacturer.*

Creation is the proof of the *Creator.*

Why were you born? It is an excellent question. It is a wonderful question. It is a frequent question. It is an *answerable* question. You deserve an answer. The answers exist. The answers are clear. The answers are more obvious than many realize.

The Manufacturer is God.

The Product is You.

The Manual is the Bible.

> ▶ *You were created to bring pleasure to God.* (See Revelation 4:11.)

> ▶ *You have been set apart for an exclusive purpose and reason.* "But know that the Lord hath set apart him that is godly for Himself" (Psalm 4:3).

> ▶ *You will give an account of your conduct and productivity.* "So then every one of us shall give account of himself to God" (Romans 14:12).

Every product contains more answers than we first realized. Study the car. The fact that it *moves* is proof that it has a different *purpose* than your home. Compare a baseball bat and a sandwich. The hardness of one and the softness of the other is an obvious *clue* that the purpose *differs.*

Studying your difference rather than your similarity to others will produce an incredible revelation of Wisdom. Especially regarding your Assignment—the problem you were created to solve.

Mechanics solve car problems.

Lawyers solve legal problems.

Ministers solve spiritual problems.

I had an interesting experience during a recent telephone conversation. While talking to someone very important in my life, I realized suddenly that I was merely listening. In fact, they asked me nothing. He did not ask me for my opinion, or feelings or observations. I waited patiently. Then, I thought, "Why am I even listening to this when he obviously does not want solutions or he would ask me questions?" Then it dawned on me. My *listening* was his solution. He simply needed someone to listen to his pain, discomfort, and heartache. Yes, even listening to someone hurting near you is often a marvelous therapy and solution to their problem.

Motivational speakers receive thousands of dollars to solve a problem for salesmen in a company. Effective counselors make an excellent living simply by being willing to listen patiently, thoughtfully, and consistently to their clients.

Sometimes, *words* heal.

Sometimes, *silence* heals.

Sometimes, *listening* heals.

It is important that you recognize your Assignment. It is essential that you embrace the *difference* in your Assignment. It is important that you are willing to be *mentored* for it.

Your function is *different* from others.

The *function* of others is different from yours.
Counselors provide *answers* to problems.
Comedians provide *escape* from problems.
Your Assignment is always to someone with a problem. Do not run from it. Embrace it.

Nine Exciting Benefits Of Problems

1. Problems Are The Gates To Your Significance.

2. Problems Are Wonderful, Glorious Seeds For Change.

3. Problems Link You To Others.

4. Problems Provide Your Income.

5. Problems Birth Opportunity To Reveal Your Uniqueness.

6. Problems Birth New Relationships.

7. Problems Are The Real Reason Friendships Exist.

8. Remove Problems From The Earth, And You Will Destroy Any Sense Of Significance In Humanity.

9. Problems Bring Good People Together During Bad Times.

The mechanic knows that an automobile problem is his connection to you.

The lawyer knows that a legal problem is his connection to you.

The dentist knows that a tooth problem is his connection to you.

The Problem God Created You To Solve On Earth Is Called Your Assignment.

∾2∾

MOST PEOPLE NEVER DISCOVER THEIR OWN ASSIGNMENT.

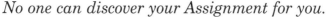

No one can discover your Assignment for you.

I read recently that the United States Department of Labor statistics revealed 70 percent of the work force of America is on the wrong job. Thousands *hate* their job. They despise getting up in the morning. They want more days off. They crave vacation time. They are unproductive, unhappy, and dissatisfied with their work. Why? They simply have not discovered their own Assignment.

God intended for you to love your work. "...to rejoice in his labour; this is the gift of God" (Ecclesiastes 5:19).

Ask yourself the *right* questions.

Answer them *honestly.* Do you drag to your job every morning? Do you delay punching in your time clock as long as possible so you can have a few extra minutes of "freedom"? Do you stretch out your lunch and coffee breaks as far as you can? Do you rush out of the building at closing time? Do you sit by the punch-out clock fifteen minutes early, anxious to get home?

If so, it is obvious that you may be working on

the wrong job. This is stealing time and money from your employer. This creates *guilt*.

Guilt always makes you critical of those in authority over you. This could explain why your life is not happy, productive or financially prosperous.

Many people never discover their own Assignment.

Six Reasons Many People Never Discover Their Own Assignment

1. *Many Do Not Even Know They Have An Assignment.* Ignorance is devastating. Millions are not exposed to hearing the Word of God daily. Millions never attend the house of God where a man of God can *unlock* their destiny.

Your destiny is often unlocked in the presence of a man of God. (Read 1 Samuel 9 and 10.) Saul knew little about his Assignment until he came into the presence of Samuel, the prophet. When he and his servant could not locate the donkeys for his father, the servant brought an *offering* to the man of God.

▶ That *Seed* was the Golden Connection to the *prophet*.

▶ The *prophet* was his Golden Link to his *destiny*.

2. *Many People Are Simply Impatient.* If it does not happen quickly, they quit. They refuse to invest the Seed of *time*.

Uncommon men have uncommon patience. A fascinating story is told in 1 Kings 18:41-45. The prophet Elijah promised King Ahab that rain was about to fall. He went up to the top of Mount Carmel, "and he cast himself down upon the earth, and put his face between his knees, And said to his servant, Go up now, look toward the sea. And he went up, and looked, and said, There is nothing. And he said, Go again seven times. And it came to pass at the seventh time, that he said, Behold, there ariseth a little cloud out of the sea, like a man's hand. And he said, Go up, say unto Ahab, Prepare thy chariot, and get thee down, that the rain stop thee not. And it came to pass in the mean while, that the heaven was black with clouds and wind, and there was a great rain" (1 Kings 18:42-45).

Elijah was powerful. What really made him powerful? Tenacity. Persistence. Determination. Unwillingness to quit. That is why he instructed his servant to look seven times. It appears that he even prayed again, and again, and again. "Elias was a man subject to like passions as we are, and he prayed earnestly that it might not rain: and it rained not on the earth by the space of three years and six months. And he prayed again, and the heaven gave rain, and the earth brought forth her fruit" (James 5:17,18).

3. *Many Succumb To Cultural Expectations Or Limited Community Opportunities.* Let me explain. Sometimes, your culture will expect women to do "women's" jobs. Men are expected to do "men's" jobs. Cultural expectations affect us. Moses was expected to continue being the general of the Egyptian army because he was the son of Pharaoh. He was raised in that culture. God had a different plan.

Though it was painful, he withdrew from his

culture and upbringing, and followed his Assignment in order to ensure long-term gain. "By faith Moses, when he was born, was hid three months of his parents, because they saw he was a proper child; and they were not afraid of the king's commandment. By faith Moses, when he was come to years, refused to be called the son of Pharaoh's daughter; Choosing rather to suffer affliction with the people of God, than to enjoy the pleasures of sin for a season; Esteeming the reproach of Christ greater riches than the treasures in Egypt: for he had respect unto the recompense of the reward. By faith he forsook Egypt, not fearing the wrath of the king: for he endured, as seeing Him who is invisible. Through faith he kept the passover, and the sprinkling of blood, lest he that destroyed the firstborn should touch them," (Hebrews 11:23-28).

It is important to overcome the limitations of community opportunities. I have had conversations with people who explained their dilemma with their Assignment. "You just do not understand, Dr. Murdock!"

Champions *create* their own opportunities.

4.   *Thousands Are Unwilling To Make Any Changes Or Leave Their Place Of Comfort In Order To Complete Their Assignment.*

The Scriptures are filled with illustrations of people who *moved* toward their geographical Assignment. Ruth left Moab and experienced her relationship with Boaz in Bethlehem. Abraham left his kinfolks. "By faith Abraham, when he was called to go out into a place which he should after receive for an inheritance, obeyed; and he went out, not knowing whither he went" (Hebrews 11:8).

5. *Most People Are Unwilling To Fight For Their Assignment.* Obedience requires warfare. Battle is normal in the life of an achiever. Thousands want to avoid confrontation with people, family, and, especially, demonic spirits.

Your Assignment will always require confrontation with someone. You have an enemy. David had Goliath.

Daniel had lions.

Esther had Haman.

Champions do warfare. "Who through faith subdued kingdoms, wrought righteousness, obtained promises, stopped the mouths of lions, Quenched the violence of fire, escaped the edge of the sword, out of weakness were made strong, waxed valiant in fight, turned to flight the armies of the aliens. Women received their dead raised to life again: and others were tortured, not accepting deliverance; that they might obtain a better resurrection: And others had trial of *cruel* mockings and scourgings, yea, moreover of bonds and imprisonment: They were stoned, they were sawn asunder, were tempted, were slain with the sword: they wandered about in sheepskins and goatskins; being destitute, afflicted, tormented; (Of Whom the world was not worthy:) they wandered in deserts, and in mountains, and in dens and caves of the earth" (Hebrews 11:33-38).

You will never be happy or satisfied until you are in the *center* of your expertise, your Assignment. This explains the incredible stories of people who left jobs worth millions for low salaries...to do exactly what they *loved*.

I read a few days ago of an attorney making $1,000,000 a year. He took a job at $30,000 a year, because it was relaxing. He now works with plants, which is what he loved all of his life. (If your hobby is more enjoyable than your work, your work should be related to your hobby.)

Fight for your Assignment. Go for it. You only have one life to live. Make your Assignment the center of your life.

6. *Many Become Obsessed With Their Weaknesses Instead Of Their Assignment.* God rebuked this in Jeremiah. "Then the word of the Lord came unto me, saying, Before I formed thee in the belly I knew thee; and before thou camest forth out of the womb I sanctified thee, and I ordained thee a prophet unto the nations. Then said I, Ah, Lord God! behold, I cannot speak: for I am a child. But the Lord said unto me, Say not, I am a child: for thou shalt go to all that I shall send thee, and whatsoever I command thee thou shalt speak" (Jeremiah 1:4-7). Jeremiah felt like a child. God instructed him not to discuss his weakness. His *Assignment* was to be his focus.

Three Important Facts About Your Weaknesses

1. *Uncommon Men Are Always Aware Of Their Weaknesses.*

Moses was obsessed with his inability to speak. So, God *staffed* his weakness by providing *Aaron*. God wanted his focus to be on his Assignment to the Israelites.

David felt uncomfortable in the armor of Saul.

So, God provided an appropriate weapon, the slingshot.

The widow of Zarephath was overwhelmed by the effects of the famine. Elijah had to remind her that the last meal she presently possessed was the Seed that would produce what she needed.

2. *Your Weakness Is An Ideal Place For God To Reveal His Supernatural Power*. "But God hath chosen the foolish things of the world to confound the wise; and God hath chosen the weak things of the world to confound the things which are mighty; And base things of the world, and things which are despised, hath God chosen, yea, and things which are not, to bring to nought things that are: That no flesh should glory in His presence. But of Him are ye in Christ Jesus, Who of God is made unto us Wisdom, and righteousness, and sanctification, and redemption" (1 Corinthians 1:27-30).

3. *The Presence And Power of God Is Always More Than Enough To Overcome Your Weakness*. "Be not afraid of their faces: for I am with thee to deliver thee, saith the Lord. Then the Lord put forth His hand, and touched my mouth. And the Lord said unto me, Behold, I have put My words in thy mouth. See, I have this day set thee over the nations and over the kingdoms, to root out, and to pull down, and to destroy, and to throw down, to build, and to plant" (Jeremiah 1:8-10).

Most People Never Discover Their Assignment.

"When Jesus Wanted To Create A
Great Miracle — He Always Gave A
Small Instruction."

- Mike Murdock -

~ 3 ~

YOUR ASSIGNMENT MAY HAVE SMALL BEGINNINGS.

Little things matter.

Small hinges control huge doors. Small keys unlock vaults containing millions of dollars. A little steering determines the direction of a huge semi-truck. One small finger dialing the telephone can start a business transaction of one billion dollars. *Never despise small beginnings.* "For who hath despised the day of small things?" (Zechariah 4:10).

Many will never achieve a great Assignment because they want their beginning to be spectacular. I am reminded of the fascinating story of Naaman, the captain of the host of the king of Syria. He was a leper. When he went to the house of Elisha, the prophet sent him a simple instruction. Elisha sent a message to him to go and wash in the Jordan River seven times. Naaman was infuriated. He had a different mental picture of how his healing would occur. One of his servants made an interesting statement, "My father, if the prophet had bid thee do some great thing, wouldest thou not have done it? how much rather then, when he saith to thee, Wash, and be clean?" (2 Kings 5:13).

The Assignment from Elisha was simple, clear, and direct. Naaman was to go wash in Jordan seven times.

When You Do The Simple, The Supernatural Occurs.

Small Beginnings Often Have Great Endings.

Jesus understood this principle. He was born in a stable. His beginning was in a small town of Bethlehem. It did not matter to Him, because He knew His destiny. He was aware of the greatness of His *destination*. One of His greatest statements ever is, "He that is faithful in that which is least is faithful also in much: and he that is unjust in the least is unjust also in much" (Luke 16:10).

Attention To Details Produces Excellence. It is the difference between extraordinary champions and losers. So, do not despise and feel insignificant in your small acts of obedience while giving birth to your Assignment.

One of the great evangelists of our day began his ministry duplicating tapes for his mentor. Hour after hour, day after day, he sat and duplicated tapes. He listened to each tape over and over. He served. He ministered. He assisted. It was the *beginning* of a significant ministry.

Ruth began as an ignorant Moabite heathen girl. Her attention to the small details of her Assignment, Naomi, positioned her as the great-grandmother of David and ushered in the lineage of Jesus.

Abigail brought lunch to the starving man, David. She became his wife.

When Jesus Wanted To Produce A Great Miracle, He Always Gave A Small Instruction.

Little things mattered to Him. Notice the small,

insignificant instructions that Jesus gave. They almost seemed ridiculous. Some might think these were instructions given to children, but none of them were. Rather, they were given to grown men, to mature adults.

"Go, wash in the pool of Siloam" (John 9:7). A big miracle? Yes, a blind man was healed from a lifetime of blindness.

"Launch out into the deep, and let down your nets for a draught" (Luke 5:4). This small instruction produced the *greatest catch of fish the disciples had ever gathered.*

"Fill the waterpots with water" (John 2:7). It produced the *greatest wine* anyone had tasted, ever. It happened at the marriage of Canaan.

"Arise, and take up thy bed, and go thy way into thine house" (Mark 2:11). What was the result? A man sick of the palsy, *immediately arose*, took up his bed, and went forth before them all and many glorified God because of it.

"Bring them hither to Me" (Matthew 14:18). These words were spoken regarding the five loaves and two fishes, the lunch of a lad. What happened afterwards has been preached around the world. *Thousands were fed miraculously*, and at the conclusion, each of the twelve disciples had a basketful to bring home!

 ▶ Great miracles do not require great instructions.
 ▶ Great miracles require *obeyed* instructions.

A student in Bible school sits in chapel daily awaiting a neon sign in the heavens declaring, "Bob, go to Calcutta, India." It never happens. Why? Bob has not obeyed the *first* instruction. "Bob, go to the prayer room at 7:00 a.m."

Obedience Turns A Common Instruction Into An Uncommon Miracle.

God does not give great instructions to great men.

God Gives Uncommon Instructions To Common Men. But when you *obey* that instruction, *greatness* is birthed. "If ye be willing and obedient, ye shall eat the good of the land" (Isaiah 1:19).

Nothing you will do today is small in the eyes of God.

Your Assignment May Have Small Beginnings.

～ 4 ～

YOUR ASSIGNMENT WAS SCHEDULED BEFORE YOUR BIRTH.

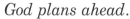

God plans ahead.

You were destined for this very time in history. Throughout the precious Scriptures, we see many illustrations of how God is involved with the unborn before a mother ever sees the face of her child.

God scheduled the birth of *Samson.* It is written, "for I have been a Nazarite unto God from my mother's womb" (Judges 16:17).

God scheduled the birth of *David.* "But thou art He that took me out of the womb: Thou didst make me hope when I was upon my mother's breasts. I was cast upon Thee from the womb: Thou art my God from my mother's belly" (Psalm 22:9,10).

God scheduled the birth of *Isaiah.* Isaiah acknowledged that it was "...the Lord that formed me from the womb to be His servant" (Isaiah 49:5).

God scheduled the birth of *John the Baptist*, "For he shall be great in the sight of the Lord, and shall drink neither wine nor strong drink; and he shall be filled with the Holy Ghost, even from his mother's womb. And many of the children of Israel shall he turn to the Lord their God" (Luke 1:15).

God scheduled the birth of *Jesus*. Jesus prayed, "Father, I will that they also, whom Thou hast given Me, be with Me where I am; that they may behold My glory, which Thou hast given Me: for Thou lovedst Me before the foundation of the world. O righteous Father, the world hath not known Thee: but I have known Thee, and these have known that Thou hast sent Me" (John 17:24,25).

God scheduled the birth of the *Apostle Paul*. "But when it pleased God, Who separated me from my mother's womb, and called me by His grace" (Galatians 1:15).

God has scheduled *your birth*. "According as He hath chosen us in Him before the foundation of the world, that we should be holy and without blame before Him in love" (Ephesians 1:4).

Yes, it is true. Samson, David, Isaiah, John the Baptist, Jesus and Paul all were chosen and called by God before their birth. Then, Paul tells you and me that God chose us prior to our birth, *even before the world was created*. This is wonderful! This is a glorious fact that you should embrace at this point in your life!

God created this *earth*.

God created *you*.

God *wanted* you *here*.

This is proof you were made *for a purpose*.

You have a *Divine* and *decided* Assignment to fulfill on the earth.

You have every right to be here.

Your Assignment Was Scheduled Before Your Birth.

❦ 5 ❦

YOUR ASSIGNMENT WILL TAKE YOU WHERE YOU HAVE NEVER BEEN BEFORE.

Changes are often uncomfortable.

When God gives you an Assignment, those seasons of discomfort are merely *bridges* to the greatest visitations of your lifetime—even if you have never been there before.

Moses went where he had never been before. Moses was sent to be the deliverer of the children of Israel. Then, God took them where none of them had *ever* gone before.

Joseph went where he had never been before. Joseph was sold by his brothers to a caravan of Ishmaelites. They sold him into Egypt, a new location and new country for him. Yet, it was there that he became second in command of the entire country.

Ruth went where she had never been before. Ruth left her native land of Moab to serve her mother-in-law, Naomi. Yes, it was a strange place and a strange lifestyle, but it was there that Ruth found the golden link to the man of her lifetime, Boaz.

Sometimes those around you are unqualified to celebrate your uniqueness. So, God takes you to *another place* where your value will be embraced and pursued.

None of these champions knew *how* God was going to direct their lives. They simply knew God. They *trusted* Him. The *will of God* mattered, as much as the *place* where He led them mattered.

Embrace this truth. *Your Assignment may take you places you never thought you would see.* Uncomfortable places. Unique places. Difficult places. I love comfort. In fact, I do not like leaving the United States at all. For several years now, I have turned down many speaking invitations I have received from all over the world because I love the comfort of predictable climates and circumstances.

A Season Of Discomfort Often Produces Rewards For A Lifetime

Many years ago, one of my dear friends, a great missionary in East Africa, wrote me a letter. "Mike, please pray about going with me to Nairobi, Kenya. We are opening up a great Christian Center. I want you to hold the first major crusade with me there."

I cannot describe for you the immense discomfort I had my first days in East Africa. I did not like the taste of the food. I did not like driving on the "wrong" side of the highway! It was almost impossible for me to use any of my American illustrations in my messages because the people would not have understood anything I said. I had to speak *slowly* so the interpreter could understand me. Occasionally, he misinterpreted my message entirely and the people did not get the message that I was delivering.

Yet, today some of the greatest memories of my life are linked to five outstanding trips to East Africa. Almost one year of my life was spent in that great country preaching the glorious gospel of Jesus Christ. In fact, a number of children over there were named after me because I was responsible for the spiritual birth of their parents.

Many years ago, I completed a crusade in Brazil and flew on to East Africa for another crusade. Concluding the crusades in East Africa, I drove all night and day in a small, cramped taxi from the interior of Tanzania to the coast. It took 14 hours. It was one of the most difficult trips of my life as I made my way into the airport, where I waited many more hours for the plane to leave for Germany. When I arrived in Germany, I had to wait more hours to fly to Poland. When I arrived in Poland, I had a six-hour ride in the back of another small taxi with all of my luggage piled high around me.

When I finally got there, after three days of flying, buried under my luggage, I preached for three hours. When I finished, the people begged me to keep going. They did not want to close the service. The secret police even came to visit the crusade and brought their families. My crusade was even held in the headquarters building of the communist party! I later learned from missionaries that the entire underground church in Poland doubled in those days of services. Here is a report I received recently from the missionary from those crusade services years ago.

"Mike, last week I returned from northern Poland, where I was invited to minister the Word of God in a church located in Lebork. The pastor of a growing church in that city, named Robert—though he was not a pastor yet when attending your meetings—and some of the people in the surrounding area were with us in Warsaw for your four-day seminar in November 1987. They gave me good reports and asked when you were coming to Poland again. Here are a couple of them:

One brother, named Kasik, who is a fisherman by occupation, told me that when you asked the people in the meeting hall to hold up their wallets believing for God's financial blessing, he held his up in faith, even though he was in debt and constantly borrowing money. *Today, he owes no man anything. He, his wife, and their five children have their own home and car!*

When Robert, the pastor, attended your seminar, we lived in a small apartment, which he shared with his brother-in-law's family. He told me that your seminar inspired him to dream of building his own home and having a car. Today he and his wife have four children. *He has a car, and I stayed in one of the rooms of the home that he built. God's Word works."*

His letter continued, "In Warsaw, you may remember, brother Andrzej, who gave to the Lord the best that he had then when picking you up from Warsaw with his old green Fiat. Since then, he has owned several vehicles, among them was a Ford

Scorpio. *Now his wife drives a Volkswagen Polo, and he has a BMW. He also owns his own large apartment.* He and his wife and three children are faithfully serving the Lord! Hallelujah!
                Do you have any plans for returning to Poland?
                                In Christ Jesus,
                                Frank J. Olszewski"

I will never forget Poland. When I walked out of the crusade that night, the Holy Spirit spoke to me and said, "There is a *place* for you, a *purpose* for you and a *people* for you." I have never experienced anything like it in my lifetime. The spiritual hunger of the Polish people is indescribable. Perhaps, they have been oppressed so long that they soak up everything they hear like a sponge. It was tremendous. I never dreamed that I would go there and share the gospel with so many hungry souls. I thank God every week for my memories of Poland.

▶ *You have not yet been everywhere God is going to take you.*

▶ You may not have even been to the place where you are going to spend the rest of your life.

▶ Be ready for *changes. Dramatic* changes. *Bold* changes. *Radical* changes. *Unexpected* changes. *Miracle* changes. *Healing* changes. *Promotional* changes.

▶ Your *greatest* friends may still be in your *future.*

▶ God is connecting you with *new people, new truth,* and *new provision.*

▶ You will not stay where you are.

Today is a temporary station where He has you changing planes.

Your Assignment Will Take You Where You Have Never Been Before.

⤳ 6 ⤳

YOUR ASSIGNMENT MAY BE TO BIRTH SOMETHING THAT HAS NEVER EXISTED BEFORE.

You were created to change somebody.

For a long time, the Jewish people had worshiped God in tents. When Solomon chose to build the Temple of the Lord, it was something that had never existed before in Israel. It was profound and awesome. Without a doubt it required uncommon faith and administrative capabilities.

Your Assignment may be so different, so extraordinary, that *no person has ever attempted it before.* If this happens, you may be tempted to become discouraged because you do not have a *pattern* before you.

Having an example is comforting. Having a role model of a champion who has done something before us can be a great motivation and encouragement.

However, God may be doing a different thing with your life—so different that He has not even entrusted your Assignment to another. *This is your season for birthing that Assignment.*

Three Essential Keys When You Receive A New Assignment

1. *Do Not Feel Obligated To Open Up Your*

Secret Longings To Everyone Near You. Your closest friends and even your family may find it impossible to encourage you in this "new adventure." Stay quiet before the Lord. Do what Mary did. Simply ponder these things in your heart.

Somebody told me that if the eggs containing little chickens are broken too quickly, the little chicks will die. So, it is with the timing of your dreams and goals. Your Assignment contains seasons. Timing is crucial. Spend time in the presence of the Holy Spirit. Permit God to give you the exact plan for your Assignment.

2. *Discern The Difference Between The Command And The Plan.*

You see, the *command* is different from the *plan*. It took a moment for Noah to get the command. But it took many years to get the plan for building the ark. It was the *first* time an ark had ever been built.

3. *Restoration Is As Necessary As Creation.*

Your Assignment may be restoration and repair. Like Nehemiah, you may be called to rebuild something that has been broken down. It may require great Seeds of patience and investment of time. Negotiation may become a major tool. You may find it disheartening that people will not rally behind you and respond to your vision.

Do not become discouraged. Your Assignment was decided by God and was discovered by you. You do not have to prove it to anyone or force other people to grasp its value. Your obedience in following His instructions will bring you great joy.

Your Assignment May Be To Birth Something That Never Existed Before.

∼ 7 ∼

YOUR ASSIGNMENT MAY APPEAR RIDICULOUS, ILLOGICAL OR EVEN IMPOSSIBLE TO OTHERS.

God never uses logic to produce miracles.

When the shepherd boy, David, faced Goliath, it appeared ridiculous. His slingshot looked like a toothpick next to the huge spear of the giant. His adolescent voice and naive countenance probably caused great laughter among the soldiers.

Even though he had killed a lion and a bear, I imagine David may have felt very uncomfortable. However, God had brought him there for a reason. He may have looked ridiculous and illogical *but God was with him. It was The Assignment.* (Read 1 Samuel 17:1-51.)

The only fact that matters is that God is with you.

It seemed impossible when Nehemiah set out to rebuild the burned and broken down walls of Jerusalem. But, somehow in the depths of his heart, Nehemiah had a mandate from God. It was not that he did not care. It was not a lack of sensitivity.

Undoubtedly, he cried himself to sleep many nights in his bed feeling like the laughing stock of the entire country. *But, it was The Assignment.* (See Nehemiah 2:12.)

The crucifixion was torturous and impossible in the mind of Jesus. He must have felt that way when He cried out in the garden "let this cup pass from me." However, God works with long-range plans, not short-term popularity contests. *It was The Assignment.* (See Matthew 26:39; 27:22-50.)

It seemed ridiculous and illogical to walk around the walls of Jericho expecting them to fall. *But that was The Assignment.* (See Joshua 6:3-5.)

It was ridiculous for Naaman the leper to expect his healing by going into the Jordan River. *But, it was The Assignment.* (See 2 Kings 5:10.)

It was illogical for a blind man to expect a miracle by washing his face. Wiping clay and spittle off his face and walking two miles to wash it off must have brought a thousand conflicting thoughts through his mind. *But, it was The Assignment.* (See John 9:6,7.)

Three Facts You Should Understand About Illogical Instructions From God

1. *Instructions From God Are Often Illogical And Ridiculous To The Human Mind.* "Because the foolishness of God is wiser than men; and the weakness of God is stronger than men. But God hath chosen the foolish things of the world to confound the wise; and God hath chosen the weak things of the world to confound the things which are

mighty...That no flesh should glory in His presence" (1 Corinthians 1:25,27,29).

2. *Illogical Instructions Are Given To Prevent Self-sufficiency And Self-worship.* "That no flesh should glory in His presence" (1 Corinthians 1:29).

3. *Uncommon Instructions Often Produce Uncommon Miracles.*

Do not despair when you receive an instruction in your prayer time that causes you to fear or dread carrying it out. Miracles are always on the other side of obedience. *Always.*

Remember, the seasons of your life will always change every time you decide to use your faith.

Your Assignment May Appear Ridiculous, Illogical Or Even Impossible To Others.

"God Never Talks To Your Logic, He
Always Talks To Your Faith."

- Mike Murdock -

≈ 8 ≈

YOUR ASSIGNMENT MAY APPEAR AT FIRST TO BE A TOTAL CONTRADICTION TO YOUR GIFTS, SKILLS AND EXPERIENCE.

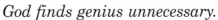

God finds genius unnecessary.

The world worships the mind. Intellectualism is the god of the age. There is a giant whirlpool of words. Men create monuments of philosophy and concepts.

God laughs.

God can use you, gifted or not. "For it is written, I will destroy the Wisdom of the wise, and will bring to nothing the understanding of the prudent. Where is the wise? where is the scribe? where is the disputer of this world? hath not God made foolish the Wisdom of this world?" (1 Corinthians 1:19,20).

Sometimes God will give you an Assignment that appears to conflict with your gifts. You may lack the educational training. It may seem unnatural and uncomfortable for you.

He wants to *grow* you. So, He will choose someone like Gideon, Jephthah or a small shepherd boy to do something astounding. "But God hath chosen the foolish things of the world to confound the wise; and God hath chosen the weak things of the world to confound the things which are mighty" (1 Corinthians 1:27).

It occurred in the life of David. He was accustomed to his little slingshot. He had been sitting with sheep on a hillside. His brothers were in battle. His father had sent him to bring food to them. As he approached the camp, he heard the shout of the huge giant, Goliath. David was not a professional soldier. He was untrained, untaught, and untried on the battlefield of war. King Saul placed his armor around David. When David took the heavy and huge sword, he was distraught. You could almost see his face contort, "I am sorry, sir! I cannot use these weapons! I cannot wear this armor. It does not even fit me."

His Assignment appears to be a total contradiction to his experience. But, God finds the genius of battle unnecessary in this particular conflict. He simply needs *access* to a pure heart. The intellectualism of generals at a strategy table is a joke to God. "That no flesh should glory in his presence" (1 Corinthians 1:29).

Moses is another example. He complained to God that he could not talk well. He was incapable of conversing with Pharaoh. God used Aaron to be a voice for him. Yet, Moses became so skilled in communicating that he wrote songs and is considered the author of the first five books of the Bible under the inspiration of the Holy Spirit.

Some of the greatest preachers who have ever lived never even attended Bible college. They were totally dependent upon the Holy Spirit. Their hearts were pure before God.

What they lacked in *social* grace, they made up in the *saving* grace of the gospel.

What they lacked in *protocol*, they possessed in *power.*

Many great and effective healing ministers have never studied a course in Divine healing. They simply had faith in God. They were swift to *obey* God. Their academic achievements were minimal. There were no long degrees behind their name. They were not obsessed with using pompous words or asking rhetorical questions.

They simply hated sickness and disease.

They knew Jesus was the Healer.

Some of the greatest singers who have ever lived never had a singing lesson. But their hearts were full. Their God-given gift craved expression. Because of this, they touched millions of lives.

When God decides your Assignment, He does not examine your past to qualify you. He examines your *heart.* "Remember ye not the former things, neither consider the things of old. Behold, I will do a new thing; now it shall spring forth; shall ye not know it? I will even make a way in the wilderness, *and* rivers in the desert" (Isaiah 43:18,19).

Focus on the future you desire, not the failure you hate. Oh, my precious friend, please receive this instruction in the depths of your heart! Do not become fearful, uncertain, and distraught at the presence of your enemy! Do not allow your weakness to become your focus. "Be not afraid of their faces: for I *am* with thee to deliver thee, saith the Lord" (Jeremiah 1:8).

Your Assignment May Appear At First To Be A Total Contradiction To Your Gifts, Skills And Experience.

"Any Miracle Will Require Your Movement From The Present."

- Mike Murdock -

∼ 9 ∼

GOD CAN GET YOU ANYWHERE HE WANTS YOU WITHIN 24 HOURS.

Miracles happen as quickly as tragedies.

The financial status of Ruth changed within 24 hours. One day Ruth, the Moabite heathen girl, is standing in a barley field. She is a peasant woman. She is impoverished. Her husband is dead. Her father-in-law is dead. Her brother-in-law is dead. Her mother-in-law is so embittered that she has changed her own name.

Suddenly, she is Mrs. Boaz.

She lives in a big house with servants waiting on her hand and foot. In the modern-day scene, chauffeurs would be opening limousine doors for her.

God can get you anywhere He wants you...within 24 hours.

The personal prestige and influence of Joseph changed within 24 hours. Joseph is in prison. Perhaps, he is wearing striped clothes and eating out of a small metal plate. He has been falsely accused of raping the wife of a government leader.

Suddenly, within 24 hours, he is seated on a throne, wearing royal robes and overseeing the entire nation of Egypt. One day he is holding a broom in his hand; the next day, he is holding a scepter. He moves from poverty to wealth...within 24 hours. In fact, he gives each of his brothers a huge piece of real estate, a ranch of their own.

God can get you anywhere He wants you within 24 hours.

The confidence and authority of the Disciples changed within 24 hours. The atmosphere is deadly. The sorrow has penetrated the homes. Jesus, the miracle worker, is gone. His body is laying in a tomb. The disciples are demoralized. Some even want to return to their fishing boats.

Suddenly, He has returned with a glorified body. He walks with them. He has a meal with them. It does not take long for incredible changes to begin. Your life can change dramatically within 24 hours.

As you obey the instructions of the Holy Spirit, you too will find miraculous turnarounds occurring. It will astonish you how quickly miracles can occur in your Assignment.

God Can Get You Anywhere He Wants You Within 24 Hours.

∾ 10 ∾

YOUR ASSIGNMENT MAY BE TO SOLVE AN EXISTING PROBLEM FOR SOMEONE WHOSE VERY SURVIVAL DEPENDS ON YOUR OBEDIENCE.

You are a life jacket to somebody close to you.

You are the *Master Key* to somebody in trouble.

Esther discovered this. When the Jewish race was threatened with extinction, Mordecai said to Esther, "who knoweth whether thou art come to the kingdom for such a time as this?" (Esther 4:14). Mordecai had discovered a secret plot by a wicked man, Haman, one of the advisers to the king. There was going to be a complete annihilation of the Jews.

So, Mordecai sent a message to Esther. He insisted that she approach the king and expose Haman's evil intention. She was frightened because her life would be endangered. Protocol required the king to summon her. She was swift to fast and wait upon God.

God honored her. Favor came from the king.

Haman was hung on the gallows and the Jews were permitted to protect themselves. Had Esther not obeyed her Assignment, thousands would have been slaughtered.

Somebody's future is always in your hands.

Joseph is a fascinating illustration. When his brothers sold him into slavery, he never became bitter. When they returned to Egypt for corn, he eventually told them who he was. He revealed that he was indeed their brother whom they had hated so long ago.

He discovered the key that released him from anxiety. He saw *every* chapter of his life as an important *ingredient* in the plan of God. "And God sent me before you to preserve you a posterity in the earth, and to save your lives by a great deliverance" (Genesis 45:7). Had Joseph not carried out his Assignment, his own family and the entire Egyptian nation would have died from starvation.

Somebody needs something God has placed within you.

Warfare is distracting.

When you focus on the *obstacles* to your Assignment, you ignore the *significance* of your Assignment. It is so easy to get wrapped up in fighting your enemy, your Goliath, that you forget there's someone close to you whose future depends on your conquering.

Somebody is observing you today.

Somebody's entire future is in your hands this very moment.

Your Assignment Is To Solve An Existing Problem For Someone Whose Very Survival Depends On Your Obedience.

≈ 11 ≈

YOUR ASSIGNMENT WILL BRING SOMEONE GREAT JOY.

Your Assignment will end a crisis for someone.

The Assignment of Jonah brought joy to 120,000 people. Read carefully the book of Jonah. God was angry. The wickedness of Nineveh had come up before Him. So, God decided to assign Jonah to that city of 120,000 people. Jonah rebelled. God decided to educate him properly in the big fish. I call it, "Seaweed University." Jonah repented and "arose, and went unto Nineveh, according to the word of the Lord" (Jonah 3:3).

The people of Nineveh believed God. They proclaimed a fast, and put on sackcloth, "...from the greatest of them even to the least of them" (Jonah 3:5).

God responded favorably. "And God saw their works, that they turned from their evil way; and God repented of the evil, that He had said that He would do unto them; and He did it not" (Jonah 3:10).

An entire city experienced miraculous joy. The Assignment of one man brought joy to an entire city.

The Assignment of David caused thousands to dance with joy in the streets of his homeland. It happened after his Assignment against Goliath. The Philistines were routed by the Israelites. Joy filled the cities, and families began to dance and shout throughout the streets. "And it came to pass as they came, when David was returned from the slaughter of the Philistine, that the women came out of all cities of Israel, singing and dancing, to meet king Saul, with tabrets, with joy, and with instruments of musick. And the women answered one another as they played, and said, Saul hath slain his thousands, and David his ten thousands" (1 Samuel 18:6,7).

▶ When a man of God *obeys,* miracles flow.
▶ When miracles flow, joy *erupts.*

The Assignment of Elijah brought joy to the heart and home of an impoverished widow. Read 1 Kings 17 for an electrifying account of Elijah's encounter with the widow of Zarephath. "And the word of the Lord came unto him, saying, Arise, get thee to Zarephath, which belongeth to Zidon, and dwell there: behold, I have commanded a widow woman there to sustain thee. So he arose and went to Zarephath. And when he came to the gate of the city, behold, the widow woman was there gathering of sticks: and he called to her, and said, Fetch me, I pray thee, a little water in a vessel, that I may drink. And as she was going to fetch it, he called to her, and said, Bring me, I pray thee, a morsel of bread in thine hand. And she said, As the Lord thy God liveth, I have not a cake, but an handful of meal in a barrel, and a little oil in a cruse: and, behold, I am gathering two sticks, that I may go in and dress it for me and my son, that we may eat it, and die" (1 Kings 17:8-12).

The widow had one meal left between her and her son. He was dying. Can you imagine her emaciated body and tortured countenance? Her son was skin and bones. Life seemed almost over for them both. It seemed that her faith had not worked. Undoubtedly, she had sung songs of confidence in God. This day, she had no song.

You are never closer to a miracle than when you receive an instruction from a man of God. "And Elijah said unto her, Fear not; go and do as thou hast said: but make me thereof a little cake first, and bring *it* unto me, and after make for thee and for thy son. For thus saith the Lord God of Israel, The barrel of meal shall not waste, neither shall the cruse of oil fail, until the day that the Lord sendeth rain upon the earth. And she went and did according to the saying of Elijah: and she, and he, and her house, did eat many days. And the barrel of meal wasted not, neither did the cruse of oil fail, according to the word of the Lord, which he spake by Elijah" (1 Kings 17:13-16).

Somewhere, a man of God received his Assignment from God. "Go to Zarephath."

His Assignment reversed the curse of hell against her life. His entry birthed a miracle.

His Assignment brought supernatural provision for the rest of the famine.

The Assignment of Queen Esther brought an entire nation great joy. Haman was an enemy of all the Jews. He had conspired against the Jews to destroy them. But, Queen Esther came before the King. She exposed his wicked plans. The Jews were allowed to "gather themselves together, and to stand for their life, to destroy, to slay, and to cause to perish, all the power of the people and province that would assault them, both little ones and women, and to take the spoil of them for a prey" (Esther 8:11).

Joy filled the cities. "The Jews had light, and gladness, and joy, and honour" (Esther 8:16).

The Assignment of Joseph brought joy to a starving nation. Joseph became the prime minister of Egypt, second in power only to Pharaoh. Imagine the great joy he brought to his father and brothers when he provided them housing, food, and access to him by bringing them into Egypt with him!

Your Assignment will bring someone great joy.

So, be willing to face your enemy. Confront your critics. Endure the season of overload. Your own Assignment may not appear to be very significant at this time. Your mind may be a whirlpool of options and choices to make. You may toss and turn at night, wondering how you are going to feed your own children and make your car payment. Begin completing the Assignment closest to your heart. Listen carefully to the Holy Spirit.

Each act of obedience will create a new wave of blessing around you. Those you love will reap ten thousand times from your obedience to God.

Seasons *change.* Your present season may be extremely difficult. It may seem to stretch every fiber of your being. You may even feel like giving up, quitting, and walking away from your Assignment. Do not do it. Joy is too close to give up now! "Weeping may endure for a night, but joy cometh in the morning" (Psalm 30:5).

Your Assignment Will Bring Someone Great Joy.

☞ 12 ☞

IF YOU REBEL AGAINST YOUR ASSIGNMENT, YOU EXPOSE YOUR ENTIRE FAMILY TO POSSIBLE LOSS AND TRAGEDY.

Everything you do is a Seed.

Your obedience will create waves of *blessing.* Your *disobedience* will create waves of pain. The Word of God confirms this truth. "If ye be willing and obedient, ye shall eat the good of the land: But if ye refuse and rebel, ye shall be devoured with the sword: for the mouth of the Lord hath spoken it" (Isaiah 1:19,20).

My father has always had a deep fear of offending God. So, I was taught this principle through the Word of God and through my father. To this very day, I have never heard my father utter a negative remark against any man of God. Some have wronged him. Some have embarrassed him publicly. Yet my father would never raise his hand or his voice against them.

There is a guaranteed reaction from God against anyone who touches His anointed. My father always believed that. "Who art thou that judgest another man's servant? to his own master he standeth or falleth" (Romans 14:4). As my mother would always say, "They will have to give an account of themselves before God."

Disobedience always produces pain. There is an interesting story in the Old Testament where Korah and 250 members of his family rebelled against Moses, the Man of God. They refused to follow the man God had assigned over their life. Korah was a rebel. He did not like Moses' leadership. He disagreed with his decisions. Instead of quietly entering the prayer closet, and pouring out his heart to God, he stirred up opposition to Moses.

He refused to focus on his Assignment of supporting the man of God.

His entire family paid dearly for his rebellion.

God opened up the earth and destroyed them. When many of his friends came to Moses and complained the next day, the wrath of God went forth *again.* The plague broke out among them and killed more than 14,000. (See Numbers 16:1-35.)

If you refuse to carry out your Assignment, your entire family may be ushered into a season of tragedies. Stay faithful to God. Stay faithful to your Assignment. Too much is at stake. Too many miracles are ahead. Too much pain can be produced through a single act of disobedience.

If You Rebel Against Your Assignment, You Expose Your Entire Family To Possible Loss And Tragedy.

☞ 13 ☜

YOUR ASSIGNMENT WILL ALWAYS INVOLVE SEASONS OF SERVANTHOOD.

━━━━━━●▶-O-◀●━━━━━━

Every successful person has served someone very well.

13 Facts About Servanthood

1.   *Jesus Taught Servanthood.* He made a fascinating statement: "The disciple is not above his master, nor the servant above his Lord" (Matthew 10:24).

2.   *Joseph Excelled In Servanthood.* First, he served Potiphar. Then, when he was falsely accused by his master's wife and thrown into jail, he served in the prison until he became the head. When he was released and promoted, he then served Pharaoh as prime minister of the nation.

Joshua served Moses. Esther served the king. Jonathan served David. Elisha served Elijah. Ruth served Naomi.

3.   *Servanthood Is The Golden Gate To Uncommon Promotion.* There is a reason for the chain of authority.

There is a reason for obedience. The purpose of supervision is not restraint, but promotion.

4. *You Can Only Be Promoted By Someone Whose Instructions You Have Followed.*
When God established the chain of authority, He was not trying to restrict, restrain, and confine you. He was not trying to stop your flexibility, destroy your creativity and imprison you.

5. *Whoever God Has Assigned Over You Becomes Qualified To Promote You.* That is the purpose of accountability.

6. *Someone Is Qualified As The Golden Connection To Move You From Where You Are To Where You Should Be.*

7. *God Has Called You To Serve Someone.* *Who* are they? *Where* are they? *How* can you serve them better? With what kind of *attitude and spirit* do you serve them?
Serve with diligence. Diligence is immediate attention to an assigned task.

8. *The Uncommon Employee Will Increase His Personal Wealth And The Money Of His Boss.* "The hand of the diligent maketh rich" (Proverbs 10:4).

9. *The Uncommon Employee Will Always Rise To The Position Of Supervisor.* "The hand of the diligent shall bear rule" (Proverbs 12:24).

10. *The Uncommon Employee Uses Everything God Has Given Him.* "A lazy man won't even dress the game he gets while hunting, but the diligent man makes good use of everything he finds" (Proverbs 12:27, The Living Bible).

11. *The Uncommon Employee Will Always Prosper.* "...the soul of the diligent shall be made fat" (Proverbs 13:4).

12. *The Focus Of The Uncommon Employee Is On Increasing The Success Of His Boss.* "The thoughts of the diligent tend only to plenteousness" (Proverbs 21:5).

13. *The Uncommon Employee Will Always Be Pursued By Uncommon Leaders.* "Seest thou a man diligent in his business? he shall stand before kings; he shall not stand before mean men" (Proverbs 22:29).

Your Assignment Will Always Involve Seasons Of Servanthood.

"What Saddens You Is A Clue To What You Are Assigned To Heal."

Mike Murdock

——➤•◦•⬧—

≈ 14 ≈

THOSE WHO UNLOCK YOUR COMPASSION ARE OFTEN THOSE TO WHOM YOU ARE ASSIGNED.

Compassion is the intense desire to heal the hurting.

Someone has said, "Compassion is the irresistible urge to rid a problem for someone."

Six Facts You Should Know About The Force Of Compassion

1.   *Jesus Had Great Compassion Toward The Sick.* "And Jesus, moved with compassion, put forth His hand, and touched him, and saith unto him, I will; be thou clean. And as soon as He had spoken, immediately the leprosy departed from him, and he was cleansed" (Mark 1:41,42).

Compassion *moves* toward someone.

Compassion *restores* the broken.

Compassion *heals*.

2.   *Jesus Had Compassion Toward Those Who Were Spiritually Confused, Wasted And Bewildered.* "And Jesus, when He came out, saw much people, and was moved with compassion toward them, because they were as sheep not having a shepherd: and He began to teach them many things" (Mark 6:34).

Compassion *discerns* the wounded.

Compassion causes you to *reach*.

Compassion births *feelings*.

3. *Compassion Can Preserve A Life.* It did for Moses when he was just a baby. "And the daughter of Pharaoh came down to wash herself at the river; and her maidens walked along by the river's side; and when she saw the ark among the flags, she sent her maid to fetch it. And when she had opened it, she saw the child: and, behold, the babe wept. And she had compassion on him, and said, This is one of the Hebrews' children" (Exodus 2:5,6).

4. *Those Who Unlock Your Compassion Are Those To Whom You Have Been Assigned.* Whose *pain* do you feel today? Whose tears do you long to wipe away? Whose sorrows keep you awake at night? This kind of compassion restores, repairs and revitalizes the life of someone close to you.

5. *Your Compassion Affects The Destiny Of Others.* "Keep yourselves in the love of God, looking for the mercy of our Lord Jesus Christ unto eternal life. And of some have compassion, making a difference: And others save with fear, pulling them out of the fire" (Jude 1:21-23).

6. *Expect The Holy Spirit To Impart Uncommon Compassion For Your Assignment.* Strongly resist complacency. Ask the Holy Spirit for a special compassion for those to whom you are assigned. He will give it to you. "Brethren, if a man be overtaken in a fault, ye which are spiritual, restore such an one in the spirit of meekness; considering thyself, lest thou also be tempted. Bear ye one another's burdens, and so fulfil the law of Christ" (Galatians 6:1,2).

Those Who Unlock Your Compassion Are Often Those To Whom You Are Assigned.

☞ 15 ☜

AN UNCOMMON ASSIGNMENT WILL REQUIRE UNCOMMON PASSION.

Passion is desire.

It includes the desire to change, serve or achieve a goal.

Men who succeed greatly possess great passion for their Assignment. They are consumed and obsessed. It burns within them like fire. Nothing else matters to them but the completion of the instructions of God in their lives.

Isaiah was passionate. "For the Lord God will help me; therefore shall I not be confounded: therefore have I set my face like a flint, and I know that I shall not be ashamed" (Isaiah 50:7).

The Apostle Paul was passionate. "Brethren, I count not myself to have apprehended: but this one thing I do, forgetting those things which are behind, and reaching forth unto those things which are before, I press toward the mark for the prize of the high calling of God in Christ Jesus" (Philippians 3:13,14).

Jesus was passionate about completing and finishing His Assignment on earth. "Looking unto Jesus the Author and Finisher of our faith; Who for the joy that was set before Him endured the cross, despising the shame, and is set down at the right hand of the throne of God. For consider Him that endured such contradiction of sinners against Himself, lest ye be wearied and faint in your minds" (Hebrews 12:2,3).

You are instructed to develop a passion for the Word of God. The Lord spoke to Joshua about the Law and instructed him to "turn not from it to the right hand or to the left, that thou mayest prosper whithersoever thou goest. This book of the law shall not depart out of thy mouth; but thou shalt meditate therein day and night, that thou mayest observe to do according to all that is written therein: for then thou shalt make thy way prosperous, and then thou shalt have good success" (Joshua 1:7,8).

So, move toward His presence today. Habitually schedule time in The Secret Place. "He that dwelleth in The Secret Place of the most High shall abide under the shadow of the Almighty" (Psalm 91:1). In His presence, your passion for Him will grow from a tiny acorn to a huge oak within you.

Wrong relationships will weaken your passion for your Assignment for God. Recently, I went to dinner with several friends after a service. Within one hour, the discussion had become filled with the problems with people, financial difficulties, and complaining attitudes. I was shocked at what began to grow within me. Though I had left the service with great joy, something began to die within me. As others discussed the difficult situations in their lives or how difficult it was to reach their goals, I felt my own fire begin to go out. Paul warned of such associations. "Be not deceived: evil

communications corrupt good n
Corinthians 15:33).

Protect the Gift of Passion within you.
your focus every hour. Be ruthless with distractions.
Feed the picture of your goal continually. Watch for
the Four Enemies of Passion: fatigue, busyness,
overscheduling, and putting God last on your daily
schedule.

An Uncommon Assignment Will Require Uncommon Passion.

"Submission Does Not Begin Until
Agreement Ends."

- Mike Murdock -

❧ 16 ❧

YOUR ASSIGNMENT WILL REQUIRE SEASONS OF SUBMISSION TO SOMEONE.

You must serve somebody.

Submission is the most misunderstood doctrine of the entire Bible.

Here Are 25 Powerful Facts About Submission

1.   *Submission Is The Willingness To Embrace The Leadership Of Those Responsible For Governing Our Lives.*

2.   *You Are Commanded To Submit To The Word Of God And The Chain Of Authority It Teaches.* The Scriptures are "...able to make thee wise unto salvation through faith which is in Christ Jesus...That the man of God may be perfect, throughly furnished unto all good works" (2 Timothy 3:15,17). "If ye be willing and obedient, ye shall eat the good of the land" (Isaiah 1:19).

3.   *Submission Is A Personal Choice.* "God resisteth the proud, but giveth grace unto the humble. Humble yourselves in the sight of the Lord, and He shall lift you up" (James 4:6,10).

4. *Submission Reveals Humility.* Some people assume that leadership is strength, and submission implies weakness. However, true submission is evidence of flexibility, trust, and humility. It is the quality of champions.

Submission is proof of humility. Humility is the gate to promotion. "Humble yourselves therefore under the mighty hand of God, that He may exalt you in due time" (1 Peter 5:6).

5. *Submission Is Your Personal Gift Of Cooperation To Those Who Govern You.* Every great leader began as a great follower. They honored authority established by God. "Obey them that have the rule over you, and submit yourselves: for they watch for your souls, as they that must give account, that they may do it with joy, and not with grief: for that *is* unprofitable for you" (Hebrews 13:17). It was *not* their weakness that made them easy to govern. Rather, it was their deep *understanding* of the laws of promotion. "Seest thou a man diligent in his business? He shall stand before kings; he shall not stand before mean men" (Proverbs 22:29).

6. *Jesus Himself Knew The Rewards Of Submission.* When He prayed in the Garden of Gethsemane, He prayed this prayer before Calvary. "O My Father, if it be possible, let this cup pass from Me: nevertheless not as I will, but as Thou wilt" (Matthew 26:39).

7. *Submission Always Results In Inner Joy.* "Looking unto Jesus the Author and Finisher of our faith; Who for the joy that was set before Him endured the cross, despising the shame, and is set down at the right hand of the throne of God" (Hebrews 12:2).

8. *Elisha Obeyed And Submitted To His Mentor, Elijah.* He received a double portion of Elijah's anointing as a reward.

9. *Those Who Refuse To Submit To The Chain Of Authority Experience Seasons Of Tragedy.* "But if ye refuse and rebel, ye shall be devoured with the sword: for the mouth of the Lord hath spoken it" (Isaiah 1:20).

10. *Submission To The Spirit Of God Produces Prosperity.* "And he sought God in the days of Zechariah, who had understanding in the visions of God: and as long as he sought the Lord, God made him to prosper" (2 Chronicles 26:5).

11. *Prosperity Always Follows Submission To An Instruction From A True Man Or Woman Of God.* "Believe in the Lord your God, so shall ye be established; believe His prophets, so shall ye prosper" (2 Chronicles 20:20).

12. *The Word Of God Commands Submission To Wise And Qualified Spiritual Leadership.* "Remember them which have the rule over you, who have spoken unto you the Word of God: whose faith follow, considering the end of their conversation" (Hebrews 13:7).

13. *Children Are Commanded To Submit To Parents.* The Apostle Paul emphasizes this. "Children, obey your parents in the Lord: for this is right. Honour thy father and mother; which is the first commandment with promise; That it may be well with thee, and thou mayest live long on the earth" (Ephesians 6:1-3). Longevity is promised. Health is promised. "Children, obey your parents in all things: for this is well pleasing unto the Lord" (Colossians 3:20).

14. *Submission To Parental Authority Guarantees Lifetime Blessing.* "Honour thy father and thy mother: that thy days may be long upon the land which the Lord thy God giveth thee" (Exodus 20:12).

15. *Fathers Must Submit To The Standard Of The Word Of God In Rearing Their Children.* Fathers are instructed, "...provoke not your children to wrath: but bring them up in the nurture and admonition of the Lord" (Ephesians 6:4).

16. *Wives Are Instructed To Submit Themselves To The Spiritual Authority Of Their Husbands.* "Wives, submit yourselves unto your own husbands, as unto the Lord. For the husband is the head of the wife, even as Christ is the head of the church: and He is the saviour of the body. Therefore as the church is subject unto Christ, so let the wives be to their own husbands in every thing" (Ephesians 5:22-24).

17. *Employees Are Instructed To Have A Submissive Attitude Toward Their Bosses.* "Servants, be obedient to them that are your masters according to the flesh, with fear and trembling, in singleness of your heart, as unto Christ; Not with eyeservice, as menpleasers; but as the servants of Christ, doing the will of God from the heart; With good will doing service, as to the Lord, and not to men" (Ephesians 6:5-7). God guarantees then, that what you make happen for others, He will make happen for you. "Knowing that whatsoever good thing any man doeth, the same shall he receive of the Lord, whether he be bond or free" (Ephesians 6:8).

18. *The Word Of God Commands Our Submission In Honoring And Respecting One*

Another. "Submitting yourselves one to another in the fear of God" (Ephesians 5:21). "Whosoever therefore shall humble himself as this little child, the same is greatest in the kingdom of heaven" (Matthew 18:4).

19. *Humble Submission Guarantees Uncommon Provision.* "By humility and the fear of the Lord are riches, and honour, and life" (Proverbs 22:4).

20. *The Scriptures Document Those Rewarded For Submission.* Ruth was submissive to Naomi. Ruth told her, "...whither thou goest, I will go; and where thou lodgest, I will lodge: thy people shall be my people, and thy God my God: Where thou diest, will I die, and there will I be buried: the Lord do so to me, and more also, if ought but death part thee and me" (Ruth 1:16,17). It was her Golden Link to Boaz, the provider and husband of her life.

21. *Your Submission To Authority Is Often Reproduced In Those Who Serve You.* David honored Saul, king of Israel. Likewise, his own men proved to be incredibly loyal and steadfast in following him. *What you are, you will create around you.* When you submit to those over you, it motivates those under *your* rule to submit to you as well. You become their example.

22. *The Submission Of Parents To Authority Directly Affects The Behavior Of Their Children.*

Just a brief note to parents: When your child sees a radar detector on the dash of your car, it is a monument to your personal rebellion to law. It will be almost impossible to persuade your children to submit to your government and authority when you obviously had no respect for law and authority over your own life.

23. *Joshua Was Loyal And Submissive To Moses.* The Israelites observed this. It affected them after the death of Moses. They spoke to Joshua, "And they answered Joshua, saying, All that thou commandest us we will do, and whithersoever thou sendest us, we will go. According as we hearkened unto Moses in all things, so will we hearken unto thee: only the Lord thy God be with thee, as He was with Moses" (Joshua 1:16,17).

24. *Employers Are Instructed To Submit To The Authority And Standards Of God.* "And, ye masters, do the same things unto them, forbearing threatening: knowing that your Master also is in heaven; neither is there respect of persons with Him" (Ephesians 6:9).

25. *Those Who Govern You Are Under The Authority Of God As Well.* Husbands are commanded to treat their wives as Christ treated the church. "Husbands, love your wives, even as Christ also loved the church, and gave Himself for it;...So ought men to love their wives as their own bodies. He that loveth his wife loveth himself. For no man ever yet hated his own flesh; but nourisheth and cherisheth it, even as the Lord the church" (Ephesians 5:25,28,29).

Your Assignment Will Require Seasons Of Submission To Someone.

☞ 17 ☜

GOD OFTEN USES SOMEONE IN AUTHORITY OVER YOU TO ADVANCE YOUR ASSIGNMENT.

Authority is *not* permission to *dominate.*

Authority *is* permission to *promote*.

The purpose of authority is not merely to restrict, but rather to advance another, to recognize and reward their obedience.

Authority requires qualification.

Authority Should Offer Three Rewards To Those Who Decide To Cooperate, Obey, Follow, Or Submit

1. *Qualified Authority Should Offer Protection To You.* God did for Israel. "And I will rebuke the devourer for your sakes, and he shall not destroy the fruits of your ground; neither shall your vine cast her fruit before the time in the field, saith the Lord of hosts" (Malachi 3:11).

Note that God did not simply instruct us to bring the tithe to Him. He promised to *protect* everything we create and generate. The covenant rewards everyone involved.

Fathers are commanded to *protect their families* and children, not merely to give them instructions and commands.

Ministers are commanded to *protect their flock,* not simply to instruct them to bring offerings to Sunday morning services.

Counselors provide protection. "Where no counsel is, the people fall: but in the multitude of counsellors there is safety" (Proverbs 11:14).

The government that requires taxes is then obligated to provide *military protection* for its citizens. If it is permissible for the government to tax my property, then the government should provide quality highways and roads.

2. *Qualified Authority Should Produce Provision For You.* That is exactly what God promised. "If thou shalt hearken diligently unto the voice of the Lord thy God, to observe and to do all His commandments which I command thee this day...The Lord shall command the blessing upon thee in thy storehouses, and in all that thou settest thine hand unto...And the Lord shall make thee plenteous in goods, in the fruit of thy body, and in the fruit of thy cattle, and in the fruit of thy ground...The Lord shall open unto thee His good treasure, the heaven to give the rain unto thy land in His season, and to bless all the work of thine hand: thou shalt lend unto many nations and thou shalt not borrow" (Deuteronomy 28:1,8,11,12).

Fathers are commanded to produce financial provision. It is important that the father who enjoys headship of his family also remember he is required by God to provide financially for every member of that family. "But if any provide not for his own, and specially for those of his own house, he hath denied the faith, and is worse than an infidel" (1 Timothy 5:8).

Ministers are commanded to produce spiritual provision. Ministers, it is not enough for you to receive the offerings and tithes of the people. You are required by God to be the *spiritual* provider in their life. "Should not the shepherds feed the flocks? Ye eat the fat, and ye clothe you with the wool, ye kill them that are fed: but ye feed not the flock. The diseased have ye not strengthened, neither have ye healed that which was sick, neither have ye bound up that which was broken, neither have ye brought again that which was driven away, neither have ye sought that which was lost; but with force and with cruelty have ye ruled them. And they were scattered, because there is no shepherd: and they became meat to all the beasts of the field, when they were scattered. My sheep wandered through all the mountains, and upon every high hill: yea, my flock was scattered upon all the face of the earth, and none did search or seek after them" (Ezekiel 34:2-6).

3. *Qualified Authority Should Promote You.* Obviously, the true source of every promotion is God, who honors a broken and contrite spirit. "The sacrifices of God are a broken spirit: a broken and a contrite heart, O God, thou wilt not despise" (Psalm 51:17).

"For promotion cometh neither from the east, nor from the west, nor from the south. But God is the judge: He putteth down one, and setteth up another" (Psalm 75:6,7).

Those who rule over you are instructed to reward you. "Withhold not good from them to whom it is due, when it is in the power of thine hand to do it" (Proverbs 3:27).

Submission is always rewarded, when it is according to the Word of God.

So, your Assignment will contain many different seasons. Do not be weary when you feel stressed, overwhelmed, and incapable of meeting the requirements others. "And let us not be weary in well doing: for in due season we shall reap, if we faint not" (Galatians 6:9).

Reaping days are coming. They will be the greatest days of your life.

God Often Uses Someone In Authority Over You To Advance Your Assignment.

⁓ 18 ⁓

ANY LEADER WHO WILLFULLY HINDERS YOUR ASSIGNMENT WILL BE JUDGED BY GOD.

God sees everything.

God will judge cruel spiritual leadership. "Thus saith the Lord God; Behold, I am against the shepherds; and I will require My flock at their hand, and cause them to cease from feeding the flock; neither shall the shepherds feed themselves any more; for I will deliver My flock from their mouth, that they may not be meat for them" (Ezekiel 34:10).

I have a wonderful word for you who have experienced cruel rulership at the hands of a spiritual despot or tyrant: God is coming toward you today. He will not leave you damaged and broken in the hands of a cruel father, husband or spiritual leader. This is what He promised:

▶ Behold, I, even I, will both search My sheep, and seek them out. As a shepherd seeketh out his flock in the day that he is among his sheep that are scattered; so will I seek out My sheep, and will deliver them out of all places where they have been scattered in the cloudy and dark day.

▶ I will bring them out from the people, and gather them from the countries, and will bring them to their own land, and feed them upon the mountains of Israel by the rivers, and in all the inhabited places of the country.

▶ I will feed them in a good pasture, and upon the high mountains of Israel shall their fold be: there shall they lie in a good fold, and in a fat pasture shall they feed upon the mountains of Israel.

▶ I will feed My flock, and I will cause them to lie down, saith the Lord God.

▶ I will seek that which was lost, and bring again that which was driven away, and will bind up that which was broken, and will strengthen that which was sick. (See Ezekiel 34:11-16).

Never follow unqualified leadership. It is possible that teachings about submission have left a bitter taste in your mouth. I have experienced that in my personal life. I have known men who were in authority over me who never took the time to hear my cries, dry my tears, and heal my wounds. It birthed bitterness at various seasons of my personal life and ministry.

I experienced a broken marriage many years ago. It was quite interesting to observe that men who wanted me to tithe from my ministry to their organization, never telephoned me, wrote me, or

See "The Assignment, Volume 2: The Anointing and The Adversity."

came to my court hearing. They merely wanted to rule me and extract from me financially and emotionally. When I was devastated and left on the road, they refused to become The Good Samaritan in my life.

They disqualified themselves to rule over me.

I am so thankful that I experienced the precious visitation and companionship of the Holy Spirit. I have learned so much in submitting to Him on a daily and hourly basis. Jesus prayed to the Father, and the Father asked the Holy Spirit to come. The Holy Spirit accommodated both the desires of the Son and the Father. That kind of ministry attitude is the force that brings reward, promotion, and provision from God.

Stop for a moment. Reconsider the direction you are going with your life. *Make a quality decision to follow quality leadership around you.* When you do, you will experience the supernatural one-hundredfold blessing that Jesus promised. (See Mark 10:28-30).

Your best days are ahead as you yield to the authority of God and spiritual leadership in your life. Walls of protection will be built by the Holy Spirit around your life. Your children will rise up to call you blessed. Those who rule over you will promote and reward you. You will taste the greatest chapters you have ever known in the coming days. God *promised* it. "And I will make them and the places round about My hill a blessing; and I will cause the shower to come down in his season; there shall be showers of blessing. And the tree of the field shall yield her fruit, and the earth shall yield her increase, and they shall be safe in their land, and shall know that I am the Lord" (Ezekiel 34:26,27).

Any Leader Who Willfully Hinders Your Assignment Will Be Judged By God.

≈ 19 ≈

YOUR ASSIGNMENT MAY ATTRACT PEOPLE WITH WRONG MOTIVES.

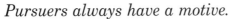

Pursuers always have a motive.

Sometimes, it is pure. Sometimes, it is not!

Whatever it is, uncover it.

When someone shows warmth and kindness at an unexpected time, it often strengthens us. It makes us feel special, celebrated, and treasured. But I have learned through difficult times that when someone is excessively congenial toward you, there is sometimes a hidden and impure motive behind it.

It happened to me a few days ago. An urgent telephone call came. Since I had not heard from this friend in almost two years, I decided to make his telephone call a priority. I accepted the call.

"Hello, Mike! I just had you on my mind for the last two weeks. I was just wondering how your ministry is going. How are you doing? Where have you been?"

As he spoke, my mind was moving swiftly. Why is he calling me just to ask me about my ministry? He has never sown one single cent into my ministry. He never writes. He has not attended one of my services in more than seven years. Why this sudden *deluge* of friendliness? I kept listening. Then, I decided to end the conversation because I had an incredible list of things to do before leaving for a crusade.

He interrupted me. "Oh, I just wanted to mention something to you." When he finished, I felt stupid, taken, and had. He simply wanted me to give some money to one of his friends. In fact, he wanted me to give a large amount of money to them for a project I knew nothing about. Absolutely nothing.

This may sound peculiar, but I absolutely felt dirty, a bit sick inside. Something inside me never wanted to hear from him again. You see, he was not genuinely interested in my ministry. He used the warm words to set me up.

It occurs quite often in life. You must confront it honestly. Name it for what it is.

Recently a well-known personality kept telephoning. He had not called me in years. And, he had never called without a reason, a motive. He gushed with praise of my ministry and work. I listened intently. "I need to meet and talk to you face to face." Something told me inside what it was. And, I was not wrong. He was involved in a multi-level marketing program, and wanted my involvement and influence.

"You know *everybody*. I could make you a fortune," he said excitedly.

He never pursued an understanding of my anointing, mantle or Assignment. Not once did he ask me what he could do to help me reach my own goals and dreams. He had his own agenda. I explained that my obsession was knowing the Holy Spirit. The Secret Place had become my focus. I wanted to spend the rest of my life writing in books what the Holy Spirit was teaching me in The Secret Place.

I have not received a phone call from him since.

Many years ago, someone rushed up to me after a conference. They were syrupy, full of flattery and warm words. I did not know them at all. But, within thirty minutes, the motive appeared.

"I understand that you sponsored a music album for a friend of mine!"

"Yes, I did," I replied slowly. "It was $25,000 cash from my pocket," I said. "It was a Seed into their ministry."

"Well, I would like for you to do the same thing for me! I want to make an album. It is my life long dream. Could you give me $25,000?"

I sat there stunned. What kind of audacity and boldness is this? How brassy can people become?

There was not one mention of even borrowing the money and repaying it. They wanted it. They thought I had it. So, "give it to me."

Always be cautious concerning the hidden agendas of those who pursue you.

> ▶ "Meddle not with him that flattereth with his lips" (Proverbs 20:19).
> ▶ "A man that flattereth his neighbour spreadeth a net for his feet" (Proverbs 29:5).
> ▶ "The Lord shall cut off all flattering lips" (Psalm 12:3).
> ▶ "A flattering mouth worketh ruin" (Proverbs 26:28).

The Apostle Paul despised flattering words and wrong motives. "For neither at any time used we flattering words, as ye know...Nor of men sought we glory, neither of you, nor yet of others, when we might have been burdensome, as the apostles of Christ. But we were gentle among you, even as a nurse cherisheth her children" (1 Thessalonians 2:5-7).

I have had quite a bit of exposure in the area of gospel music. Because I know artists who record songs, it has been a normal occurrence to have someone shove cassettes and sheet music into my hands and say, "God told me that you are my connection to this artist. Will you see that they receive this and tell them about me?" This has occurred on many occasions.

Now, I am a musician. I am a song writer. So, I understand the desire for others to sing my songs. But, my Assignment to help people has attracted some with *wrong* motives. It is my personal responsibility to test, qualify, and discern their true intent and motives.

It happened to Peter and John. Read the complete fascinating story in Acts 8. Simon, who had practiced sorcery "...himself believed also: and when he was baptized, he continued with Philip, and wondered, beholding the miracles and signs which were done" (Acts 8:13).

But, wrong motives entered.

"And when Simon saw that through laying on of the apostles' hands the Holy Ghost was given, he offered them money, Saying, Give me also this power, that on whomsoever I lay hands, he may receive the Holy Ghost" (Acts 8:18,19).

Peter had discerned Simon's wrong motive. "For

I perceive that thou art in the gall of bitterness, and in the bond of iniquity" (Acts 8:23).

Peter reacted to wrong motives in a strong, decisive, and dramatic way. "But Peter said unto him, Thy money perish with thee, because thou hast thought that the gift of God may be purchased with money. Thou hast neither part nor lot in this matter: for thy heart is not right in the sight of God. Repent therefore of this thy wickedness, and pray God, if perhaps the thought of thine heart may be forgiven thee" (Acts 8:20-22).

After a crusade service one night, my assistant handed me a business card. It was from a wealthy man with a very successful business. My assistant explained, "He has heard about the results of your prayers for the prosperity of Christian business people. He has heard of your anointing with oil the door posts of businesses, and asking God's blessing upon that place. He pulled out a huge stack of money and wanted me to give it to you if you would come pray over his business."

"You know that I will not do that," was my reply.

"I told him that. He said you could name your price, and he would pay you whatever you want, to pray over his business."

I threw the card away.

My prayers are not "for sale".

My faith will not be prostituted.

My confidence in God cannot be merchandised.

If there is an anointing that flows through your life, it will have a *magnetism.** Unfortunately, it often attracts wrong people as well as deserving individuals.

You may have a special mantle of financial

blessing on your life. Perhaps, you are a paymaster for the kingdom, one of those persons who God touches and causes great wealth to flow through your hands to touch many lives. It is important that you understand the magnetism, appeal, and drawing power your money has with many. One of the wealthiest men who ever lived wrote, "The poor is hated even of his own neighbour: but the rich hath many friends" (Proverbs 14:20). He insisted again, "Wealth maketh many friends; but the poor is separated from his neighbour" (Proverbs 19:4).

During the last several years, I have received letters from various ministers, musicians, and aggressive achievers who wrote me, "I would like for you to recommend me to be on this particular television show. I know they are friends of yours. Would you introduce me?"

When I failed to respond, I never heard from them again. To them, I was merely a "stepping stone" on the way to their future.

Please understand, I *love* sowing into the lives of worthy people. I *love* giving. It is a powerful part of my nature. In fact, I give away thousands of books and tapes each month. It is a Law of Blessing. Jesus guaranteed one hundredfold return for anything given up for the sake of the gospel. (See Mark 10:28-30.)

The giving of gifts can even conceal hidden agendas. Unfortunately, satan has often used giving as a weapon of manipulation. It happened some months ago. I suddenly received in the mail a very expensive and exquisite gift from someone who had never written me, never given me anything, nor attended my meetings. I pondered on this.

A few weeks later, my secretary approached me and said, "You received a telephone call from someone who wants to meet with you." I realized that the purpose of the gift was to soften me up for the meeting. This is unfortunate. It is ungodly. It is wrong. "A wicked man taketh a gift out of the bosom to pervert the ways of judgment" (Proverbs 17:23).

When a gift is given from a pure heart to honor another, it prospers the relationship. It prospers the *sower*. It prospers the one who *receives*. "A gift *is as* a precious stone in the eyes of him that hath it: whithersoever it turneth, it prospereth" (Proverbs 17:8).

Motives should *strengthen* relationships.

Motives should *build* bridges.

Motives should *reveal* caring, compassion, and appreciation.

Your Assignment May Attract People With Wrong Motives.

"Attack Is The Proof Your Enemy Has
Confidence In Your Ability To Achieve
Your Goal."

Mike Murdock

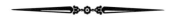

⪻ 20 ⪼

THOSE WHO SCORN YOUR ASSIGNMENT MAY SUFFER DEVASTATING LOSSES.

Your Assignment is serious to God.

It should become serious to others. God will hold them accountable for their reaction to it.

Those who scorned the Apostle Peter's ministry suffered tragedy. Let me explain. Ananias and Sapphira lost their lives after lying to Peter. It was a loss that was unnecessary and avoidable. They simply should have told the truth. (Read Acts 5:1-11.)

Those who rally opposition to spiritual leaders expose their family to the wrath of God. Korah and his family were destroyed by God when they acted in rebellion against the authority of Moses. It was avoidable. They should have been teachable. The tragedy could have been averted. (Read Numbers 16:1-40.)

Those unoffended by sin may eventually lose their ability to experience correction. Lot's wife looked back. She became a pillar of salt. That was avoidable and unnecessary. She kept her ties to the ungodly in Sodom and Gomorrah. (See Genesis 19:26.)

Those who knowingly attempt to lie to a man of

God will open the floodgates of hell against their life.
Gehazi, the servant of Elisha the man of God, had a
horrifying experience. It followed the healing of
Naaman, the leper. Naaman wanted to bless Elisha,
the man of God. After Elisha turned down the gift,
Gehazi discreetly went to Naaman and asked for the
gift. When he returned, Elisha knew in his heart
what Gehazi had done. Gehazi lied when Elisha
interrogated him about his whereabouts. Elisha
pronounced his penalty. "The leprosy therefore of
Naaman shall cleave unto thee, and unto thy Seed
for ever. And he went out from his presence a leper
as white as snow" (2 Kings 5:27).

The assistant to the prophet lost his position,
his health, and his credibility. It was unnecessary
and totally avoidable. He could have simply told
the truth.

*Those Who Scorn Your Assignment May Suffer
Devastating Losses.*

≈ 21 ≈

OBEDIENCE TO YOUR ASSIGNMENT MAY CREATE A TEMPORARY SEASON OF LOSS.

Some losses are avoidable.
Some losses are vital.
Obedience is rarely easy.

Yet, your Assignment will require many acts of obedience. Some of those instructions will create losses. However, those losses are necessary and essential for long term gains. God has *reasons* for every demand He makes upon your life.

Moses experienced the loss of status and position. "By faith Moses, when he was come to years, refused to be called the son of Pharaoh's daughter; Choosing rather to suffer affliction with the people of God, than to enjoy the pleasures of sin for a season; Esteeming the reproach of Christ greater riches than the treasures in Egypt: for he had respect unto the recompense of the reward. By faith he forsook Egypt, not fearing the wrath of the king: for he endured, as seeing him who is invisible" (Hebrews 11:24-27).

Moses saw the *bigger* picture. He saw the future. He saw the *reward*. He knew the limitations of Egypt. He knew the inevitable eventuality of *promotion*. "And let us not be weary in well doing: for in due season we shall reap, if we faint not" (Galatians 6:9).

You see, seasons change.

"To every thing there is a season, and a time to every purpose under the heaven: A time to be born, and a time to die; a time to plant, and a time to pluck up that which is planted; A time to kill, and a time to heal; a time to break down, and a time to build up; A time to weep, and a time to laugh; a time to mourn, and a time to dance; A time to cast away stones, and a time to gather stones together; a time to embrace, and a time to refrain from embracing; A time to get, and a time to lose; a time to keep, and a time to cast away" (Ecclesiastes 3:1-6).

Abraham knew the losses of comfort, friends and home. "Now the Lord had said unto Abram, Get thee out of thy country, and from thy kindred, and from thy father's house, unto a land that I will show thee" (Genesis 12:1).

Abraham was tested with the potential loss of his son of promise, Isaac. "And it came to pass after these things, that God did tempt Abraham, and said unto him, Abraham: and he said, Behold, here I am. And he said, Take now thy son, thine only son Isaac, whom thou lovest, and get thee into the land of Moriah; and offer him there for a burnt offering upon one of the mountains which I will tell thee of" (Genesis 22:1,2).

Abraham knew the loss of peaceful relationships. "And Lot also, which went with Abram, had flocks, and herds, and tents. And the land was not able to bear them, that they might dwell together: for their substance was great, so that they could not dwell together. And there was a strife between the herdmen of Abram's cattle and the herdmen of Lot's cattle: and the Canaanite and the Perizzite dwelled then in the land. And Abram said unto Lot, Let there be no strife, I pray thee, between me and thee, and between my herdmen and thy herdmen; for we be brethren. Is not the whole land before thee? Separate thyself, I pray thee, from me: if thou wilt take the left hand, then I will go to the right; or if thou depart to the right hand, then I will go to the left" (Genesis 13:5-9).

Abraham persisted in serving God through seasons of loss. "He staggered not at the promise of God through unbelief; but was strong in faith, giving glory to God; And being fully persuaded that, what He had promised, He was able also to perform" (Romans 4:20,21).

Abraham was rewarded for every loss. He became the Father of Nations. "Therefore it is of faith, that it might be by grace; to the end the promise might be sure to all the Seed; not to that only which is of the law, but to that also which is of the faith of Abraham; who is the father of us all, (As it is written, I have made thee a father of many nations) before him whom he believed, even God, who quickeneth the dead, and calleth those things which be not as though they were. Who against hope believed in hope, that he might become the father of many nations, according to that which was spoken, So shall thy Seed be" (Romans 4:16-18).

Stephen lost his life. I find the story of Stephen

fascinating. He was the first minister of helps selected by the early church. The widows were neglected. The twelve disciples asked the multitude to select seven men to handle the business of the church. The first they chose was "Stephen, a man full of faith and of the Holy Ghost...And Stephen, full of faith and power, did great wonders and miracles among the people" (Acts 6:5,8).

When Stephen spoke, conviction was so powerful that men responded with anger. "And they were not able to resist the Wisdom and the Spirit by which he spake" (Acts 6:10).

When people saw Stephen, his countenance was like an angel. "And all that sat in the council, looking steadfastly on him, saw his face as it had been the face of an angel" (Acts 6:15).

Overwhelmed with conviction, they decided to kill him. "When they heard these things, they were cut to the heart, and they gnashed on him with their teeth. Then they cried out with a loud voice, and stopped their ears, and ran upon him with one accord, and cast him out of the city, and stoned him...And they stoned Stephen, calling upon God, and saying, Lord Jesus, receive my spirit" (Acts 7:54,57-59).

Yes, he lost his life.

But look at what happened. "But he, being full of the Holy Ghost, looked up stedfastly into heaven, and saw the glory of God, and Jesus standing on the right hand of God. And he kneeled down, and cried with a loud voice, Lord, lay not this sin to their charge. And when he had said this, he fell asleep" (Acts 7:55,60).

God even rewarded Stephen at the losing of his

life. Jesus rose and stood at the right hand of the Father to welcome Stephen's entry into the glory.

The Apostle Paul experienced loss of position, prestige and influence. Let him tell the story in his own words: "Circumcised the eighth day, of the stock of Israel, of the tribe of Benjamin, an Hebrew of the Hebrews; as touching the law, a Pharisee; Concerning zeal, persecuting the church; touching the righteousness which is in the law, blameless. But what things were gain to me, those I counted loss for Christ. Yea doubtless, and I count all things but loss for the excellency of the knowledge of Christ Jesus my Lord: for Whom I have suffered the loss of all things, and do count them but dung, that I may win Christ" (Philippians 3:5-7).

You must see treasures beyond your losses.

The Double Portion Blessing Of God Can Follow Every Major Loss. It happened to Job when he lost his children, his flocks, and herds, and his position of credibility and popularity. "And the Lord turned the captivity of Job, when he prayed for his friends: also the Lord gave Job twice as much as he had before. Then came there unto him all his brethren, and all his sisters, and all they that had been of his acquaintance before, and did eat bread with him in his house: and they bemoaned him, and comforted him over all the evil that the Lord had brought upon him: every man also gave him a piece of money, and every one an earring of gold. So the Lord blessed the latter end of Job more than his beginning: for he had fourteen thousand sheep, and six thousand camels, and a thousand yoke of oxen, and a thousand she asses. He had also seven sons and three daughters. And he called the name of the first, Jemima; and the name of the second, Kezia; and the name of the third, Kerenhappuch. And in all the land were no women found *so* fair as the daughters of Job: and their father gave them inheritance among their brethren. After this lived Job an hundred and forty years, and saw his sons, and his sons' sons, even four generations. So Job died, being old and full of days" (Job 42:10-17).

Obedience To Your Assignment May Create A Temporary Season Of Loss.

≈ 22 ≈

YOUR ASSIGNMENT MAY FIRST APPEAR TO BE UNDESIRABLE AND EVEN REPULSIVE.

————➤•❖•◄————

Uncommon gifts can come in unattractive packaging.

Divinity differs from humanity.

Man sees the immediate.

God sees the *eventuality*.

"...for the Lord seeth not as man seeth; for man looketh on the outward appearance, but the Lord looketh on the heart" (1 Samuel 16:7).

Calvary was not a desirable Assignment to Jesus. Consider Jesus. He was pure, yet called to minister to the impure. He was holy, yet called to live around the unholy. He was brilliant, yet assigned to the ignorant. He was perfect, yet assigned to live with the imperfect.

Now, observe His cry as He enters the crucial part of his entire Assignment on earth, the crucifixion. He is in the Garden of Gethsemane. His disciples are asleep. It seems that God Himself has turned His back on Him, the Son. He weeps desperately, "O My Father, if it be possible, let this up pass from Me: nevertheless not as I will, but as Thou wilt" (Matthew 26:39).

Titus had a repulsive Assignment. Paul writes to him to reassure him. He knew, "the Cretans are always liars, evil beasts, slow bellies" (Titus 1:12). Then, he explains that that is the very reason why Titus was chosen and assigned to be in Crete! "For this cause left I thee in Crete, that thou shouldest set in order the things that are wanting, and ordain elders in every city, as I had appointed thee" (Titus 1:5).

Jonah despised his Assignment to Nineveh. "But Jonah rose up to flee unto Tarshish from the presence of the Lord, and went down to Joppa; and he found a ship going to Tarshish" (Jonah 1:3). Of course, the Bible is also clear about the consequences of his rebellion. He paid for it. "So he paid the fare thereof" (Jonah 1:3). As unappealing and repulsive as parts of your Assignment might appear, nothing is worse than "Seaweed University" in the bottom of the sea. Never forget this.

Jeremiah found his Assignment terribly disheartening. "Oh that I had in the wilderness a lodging place of wayfaring men; that I might leave my people, and go from them! for they be all adulterers, an assembly of treacherous men" (Jeremiah 9:2). He did not even want to stay in the ministry. He despised the low quality of the people to whom he was assigned. He preferred solitude. But, it was his Assignment.

Abraham had painful days in his Assignment. Nothing could be more devastating than an instruction he received from the Lord. "And he said, Take now thy son, thine only *son* Isaac, whom thou lovest, and get thee into the land of Moriah; and offer him there for a burnt offering upon one of the mountains which I will tell thee of" (Genesis 22:2).

This is heartbreaking, repulsive, and unexplainable. It is an Assignment that was utterly repulsive. Yet, Abraham knew God. He believed that God always had his best interests at heart.

> ▶ He obeyed *immediately* and *completely*. He "who against hope believed in hope, that he might become the father of many nations" (Romans 4:18).

> ▶ *He refused to disobey. He insisted on believing.* "He staggered not at the promise of God through unbelief; but was strong in faith, giving glory to God" (Romans 4:20).

> ▶ He was persuaded concerning *the heart and the ability of God*. "And being fully persuaded that, what He had promised, He was able also to perform" (Romans 4:21).

Three Golden Keys To Remember When Your Assignment Is Heartbreakingly Difficult

1. *When You Doubt Your Instruction, Never Doubt Your Instructor.* "Trust in the Lord with all thine heart; and lean not unto thine own understanding" (Proverbs 3:5).

2. Remember, *It Is Not The Magnetism Of Those To Whom You Are Assigned, But The Irrefutable And Undeniable, Burning Call Of God Within Your Heart, That Drives You In Your Assignment.* It burned in Jeremiah. "Then I said, I will not make

mention of Him, nor speak any more in His name. But His Word was in mine heart as a burning fire shut up in my bones, and I was weary with forbearing, and I could not stay" (Jeremiah 20:9).

3. *Always Remember That Nothing Is Ever As Bad As It First Appears.* Nothing. Beyond the crucifixion is a resurrection.

"They that sow in tears shall reap in joy. He that goeth forth and weepeth, bearing precious Seed, shall doubtless come again with rejoicing, bringing his sheaves with him" (Psalm 126:5,6).

"Weeping may endure for a night, but joy cometh in the morning" (Psalm 30:5).

▶ Beyond the lion's den is a promotion.

▶ Beyond tears, there is laughter.

Your Assignment May First Appear To Be Undesirable And Even Repulsive.

≈ 23 ≈

YOUR ASSIGNMENT MAY REQUIRE PERIODIC SEPARATION FROM THOSE YOU LOVE.

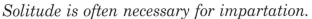

Solitude is often necessary for impartation.
It is normal to love the atmosphere of friends. Connection is essential for multiplication. It takes two to become more. "Two *are* better than one" (Ecclesiastes 4:9). *But, your Assignment will have many moments of withdrawing from others.*

Jesus withdrew Himself from the multitudes. "But so much the more went there a fame abroad of Him: and great multitudes came together to hear, and to be healed by Him of their infirmities. And He withdrew Himself into the wilderness, and prayed" (Luke 5:15,16).

"Now when Jesus saw great multitudes about Him, He gave commandment to depart unto the other side" (Matthew 8:18).

Jesus taught His followers to come apart from others for times of restoration. And He said unto them, "Come ye yourselves apart into a desert place, and rest a while: for there were many coming and going, and they had no leisure so much as to eat.

And they departed into a desert place by ship privately" (Mark 6:31,32).

Jesus withdrew from the pressure of people, knowing that ministry is emptying. Restoring others requires emptying yourself. When others reach, they draw something out of you. Jesus experienced this with the woman who had an issue of blood for twelve years. "For she said, If I may touch but His clothes, I shall be whole" (Mark 5:28). It did happen. But Jesus felt something leave Him. "And Jesus, immediately knowing in Himself that virtue had gone out of Him, turned Him about in the press, and said, Who touched My clothes?" (Mark 5:30).

▶ Sometimes, you must withdraw from the *pressure* of people.

▶ Sometimes, you must withdraw from the *pleasure* of people.

So, God will often speak to you to have moments away from those you love.

It will restore you and strengthen you.

It will also enable you to hear His voice without the stain and distortion of human logic and opinions.

Sometimes, your Assignment will cost you wonderful moments of conversation and relaxation times. It is the opposite of rest times. It will demand *all* of you. It will require your total absorption and concentration.

I am sitting in my Wisdom Room dictating this to you. There are books wall-to-wall and ceiling-to-floor. I absolutely love books. I love biographies and success books. And I love collecting new ones monthly.

Next to this room is the most important room

in my home, The Secret Place. It is a small but power-filled room dedicated to the Holy Spirit. He dramatically affected my life on July 13, 1994, and I have been a different man since that day. My yard is large, but it has speakers on the trees that play Holy Spirit music continuously.

Yet, I spend my life traveling thousands of miles every month *away from here.* I spend most of my life sleeping in strange little bedrooms in strange hotels in strange cities. I sit in a tiny cramped airplane seat for hours, with thoughts of being in my recliner in my Wisdom Room, reading!

I long to stay home. Traveling is not exciting to me any more. I have done it for more than thirty years. Then, why do I stay in cramped little hotel quarters, rushing from airport to airport just to speak for a few minutes to audiences across this globe?

It is The Assignment.

Occasionally, I feel sorry for myself. Sometimes, I envy those who wake up in the same bed every morning, eating breakfast at the same table, and seeing faithful and loyal friends every day of their lives. Sometimes, I have to remind myself that, "This world is not my home, I am just passing through. I am a pilgrim. I am a wayfarer." It is not always easy to walk away from pleasurable surroundings.

I love my staff. It has taken me thirty years to have the team of champions that surround me daily. I admire them. I respect them. They are my family. Yet, I rarely get to spend long hours and days with them. The Assignment is my obsession.

Last night, I had an intense desire to lean back and watch some videos. I was tired. I just had an incredible week of meetings. God had moved. People were radically touched and restored. I really did not want to work late last night at all. But, I looked at the letters of partners and those who had written me.

They deserved an answer. Like Jesus, "...when He saw the multitudes, He was moved with compassion on them, because they fainted, and were scattered abroad, as sheep having no shepherd" (Matthew 9:36).

Compassion is a force. A powerful force. It is something I cannot explain. When I turned 50 years old I spoke on the subject, "Fifty years: My Memories, Mistakes, and Miracles." I told my family of partners, and friends that I could not explain compassion. When you care about people, you are driven to minister to them. It is something overpowering, unexplainable, and unavoidable when you get in His presence.

Satan often exploits this compassion to drive us into achievements that God never instructed. I am very aware that some of our drive and energy can become ambition, uncontrolled and undirected by the Holy Spirit. This has happened in thousands of lives. However, it cannot be denied either that His calling can so dominate your life that you forfeit moments of pleasure and things that you would love to be doing.

Why do we withdraw from pleasurable moments from those we love? *The Harvest beckons.* "Then saith He unto His disciples, The Harvest truly *is* plenteous, but the labourers are few; Pray ye therefore the Lord of the Harvest, that He will send forth labourers into His Harvest" (Matthew 9:37,38).

One of the greatest evangelists in history told me of his deep love for the game of golf.

"How often do you go golfing?"

"Every chance I get," he answered.

"Do you go daily?" I asked.

"I would if I had the time," was his strong reply. But, he had an Assignment. He trains thousands of people for the ministry every year.

Something matters far more than our pleasure. Tomorrow will last longer than today.

> ▶ *Champions Are Willing To Do Things They Hate To Create Something They Love.*
> ▶ *Champions Make Decisions That Create Their Desired Future While Losers Make The Decisions That Create Their Desired Present.*

There is a costly season for *sowing* your life into *others*. "And Jesus saith unto him, The foxes have holes, and the birds of the air have nests; but the Son of man hath not where to lay his head" (Matthew 8:20).

There is a compensation season for *reaping* from the One who gave you your Assignment. "And let us not be weary in well doing: for in due season we shall reap, if we faint not" (Galatians 6:9).

Peter experienced aloneness. He must have felt the loneliness of withdrawing from those he loved. He missed the vibrant and exciting atmosphere of the fishing boats at times. "Then Peter began to say unto Him, Lo, we have left all, and have followed Thee" (Mark 10:28).

Jesus guaranteed reward on the other side of

separation. He made a powerful, incredible, and marvelous response. I cannot say it any better than our precious Lord said it that day: "And Jesus answered and said, Verily I say unto you, There is no man that hath left house, or brethren, or sisters, or father, or mother, or wife, or children, or lands, for My sake, and the gospel's, But he shall receive an hundredfold now in this time, houses, and brethren, and sisters, and mothers, and children, and lands, with persecutions; and in the world to come eternal life" (Mark 10:29,30).

You will never regret pursuing your Assignment.

But, it is true. *Your Assignment May Require Periodic Separation From Those You Love.*

≈ 24 ≈

YOUR ASSIGNMENT MAY REQUIRE YOU TO WALK AWAY FROM SOMETHING IMPORTANT TO YOU.

————≫•◦•≪————

Comfort is addictive.

Every tiny action in your life is always a step away from perceived *pain* or a step toward anticipated *gain*. It is normal to pursue increase, comfort, and promotion. It is normal to become attached to the things that really matter to us, such as our home, family or a cherished possession.

When God births your Assignment, it often requires you to walk away from something you want very much; a treasured friendship, a cherished possession, or even a deeply rooted belief system and philosophy.

You may be required to walk away from a proven source of income. Peter did. "And Jesus answered and said, Verily I say unto you, There is no man that hath left house, or brethren, or sisters, or father, or mother, or wife, or children, or lands, for My sake, and the gospel's, But he shall receive an hundredfold now in this time, houses, and brethren, and sisters, and mothers, and children, and lands, with ersecutions; and in the world to come eternal life," (Mark 10:29,30).

James and John walked away from their fishing business. "And going on from thence, He saw other two brethren, James the son of Zebedee, and John his brother, in a ship with Zebedee their father, mending their nets; and He called them. And they immediately left the ship and their father, and followed Him" (Matthew 4:21,22).

You may be required to leave the comfort of your home, family and relatives. Abraham did. "Now the Lord had said unto Abram, Get thee out of thy country, and from thy kindred, and from thy father's house, unto a land that I will shew thee" (Genesis 12:1).

Ruth left her home country. "And Ruth said, Intreat me not to leave thee, or to return from following after thee: for whither thou goest, I will go; and where thou lodgest, I will lodge: thy people shall be my people, and thy God my God: Where thou diest, will I die, and there will I be buried: the Lord do so to me, and more also, if ought but death part thee and me" (Ruth 1:16,17).

I understand this kind of commitment. It happens in my own life every single week. I love my Schools of the Holy Spirit hosted each month in some of the top cities of America. I love talking to pastor friends as I minister in their churches. Ministering and teaching in conferences, seminars, and crusades is a very pleasurable and wonderful Assignment on earth. However, I love my home. When I am at home, I never want to leave. In fact, I have done without meals just to avoid driving out of the driveway!

Though a major mall is fifteen minutes from my house, I would rather stay home and eat a sandwich than drive fifteen minutes to a major restaurant.

I have traveled widely, including trips to 36 nations of the world. I have seen the pyramids, the catacombs, and Mt. Kilimanjaro. I have spent many months in Africa, Switzerland, Germany, Russia, India, France, and England. The list goes on. But, I would rather be at home reading and seeking the face of God in The *Secret Place*.

Your Assignment may require you to release something important to you.

Concentrate on the Rewards of Obedience.

Now, the rewards are obvious, inevitable and consistent. And, that is really how God keeps motivating me to obey Him. "If ye be willing and obedient, ye shall eat the good of the land" (Isaiah 1:19).

Remain aware of the consequences of missing the will of God. "But if ye refuse and rebel, ye shall be devoured with the sword: for the mouth of the Lord hath spoken it" (Isaiah 1:20).

I have a healthy fear of God. It was birthed and nurtured from my childhood years. My mother constantly reminded me that "The fear of the Lord is the beginning of Wisdom" (Proverbs 9:10). I knew the rewards of Wisdom! "For by Me thy days shall be multiplied, and the years of thy life shall be increased" (Proverbs 9:11). "Riches and honour are with Me; yea, durable riches and righteousness. My fruit is better than gold, yea, than fine gold; and My revenue than choice silver...That I may cause those that love Me to inherit substance; and I will fill their treasures" (Proverbs 8:18,19,21).

The incentives are obvious and proven. So, I am willing to walk away from something important to me in order to pursue something which benefits me *more*.

God sometimes uses an experience to break your addiction to a possession, a comfort zone or even a relationship.

I remember a deeply cherished earthly possession of many years ago, a beautiful, rare gold watch. I bought it in Lausanne, Switzerland. I never saw another one like it. There were only two made like it in the world. It had a beautiful fifty carat quartz stone on top. Several friends wanted to purchase it from me. It was gorgeous. It was my point of significance from those around me!

One morning, during a season of great adversity, I rushed out the door to take some clothes to the cleaners. Because I was in a rush, I simply placed my watch on top of the shirts in my lap as I drove to the cleaners. I intended to put it on as I was driving. Something distracted me and when I arrived at the cleaners, it was still on the pile of shirts.

I rushed inside and left my clothes, and rushed on to my office. Suddenly, it dawned on me that I was not wearing my watch. I telephoned the cleaners and returned to look for it. They denied that the watch was in the cleaning. Perhaps, it fell off the shirt load as I stepped out of the car. I will never know. I was heartbroken.

Also, because of the turmoil of the court trials I was experiencing, I had neglected to keep the insurance coverage current! I could never collect on it. I felt so dead and sick inside. As I walked through my office praying quietly in the Holy Spirit, I could not believe that I had lost my most valued material possession. I valued it above my home, my car, and everything else. Suddenly, the Holy Spirit spoke a simple sentence to me. "Hold loosely to the things of this world."

I have never forgotten that sentence to this day.

I do not have a thing that did not come from the Lord anyhow.

Everything I have was *given* to me.

Everything I possess is something I have *received from Another.*

Whatever you give up in the pursuit of your Assignment, I promise you that God will repay you one hundred times over. You have *His* Word on it. "And Jesus answered and said, Verily I say unto you, There is no man that hath left house, or brethren, or sisters, or father, or mother, or wife, or children, or lands, for my sake, and the gospel's, But he shall receive an hundredfold now in this time, houses, and brethren, and sisters, and mothers, and children, and lands, with persecutions; and in the world to come eternal life" (Mark 10:29,30).

It is in the Eternal Contract of the Kingdom.

I received a disturbing telephone call several years ago. One of my college buddies had a crisis in his marriage. He felt impressed of God to accept a pastorate. His wife refused to move.

"Mike, I really love my wife and I want peace in my marriage. She refuses to accept the calling of God to this new church. What should I do?"

"I would embrace it in two ways: First, I would

permit her to be a corrective influence. God gave her to you for a reason. She is the gift of God to your life. She brings balance. Perhaps it is not the will of God for you to go to the church. Get into The Secret Place. Ask the Lord if He is using her as a corrective measure to help you stay on course. You may have a vision produced by your imagination. She may have the balance and practicality of building where you are."

I continued, "Secondly, if you go to The Secret Place and receive affirmation from the Holy Spirit that you indeed are in the will of God, embrace the challenge of teaching and mentoring her to *hear the voice of God*. Show her the rewards of obedience. Begin to nurture in her the importance of both of you following the Lord. Remind her how precious and special she is to your life. She is like the body of Christ is to Jesus. Emphasize your need for her to stand by your side."

He agreed. Some days later, the phone rang again. She was adamant. She refused to move or even consider discussion. After encouraging him to go to a marriage counselor, I entered into a prayer of agreement with him on the telephone that he would have the courage to do the will of God *regardless of the cost.*

According to a recent conversation, the family has been fragmented. He chose to stay instead of accepting the church God had spoken to him about. He is miserable and so is the entire family. He failed the test of leadership—*the willingness to do the will of God alone if necessary.*

I am persuaded your *family is important.*

I am persuaded your *mate is important.*

I am persuaded your *marriage is important.*

I am more persuaded that doing *the will of God* is the most important decision of your lifetime. *Your Assignment is more important than any other relationship in your life.* It is that invisible and overpowering calling that causes an evangelist to travel day after day, to strange airports and hotels and even away from the family who may refuse to follow him.

It is what makes a great missionary travel all over East Africa and not see his own children for many months. He loves the United States. He enjoys the pleasure of nice hotels. He cherishes the laughter of his grandchildren. But, his Assignment cannot be changed by him or anybody else. He knows it.

The price is great.

But, the peace is worth it.

Obviously, there are carnal and manipulative people who would twist the Scriptures to accommodate their own lust of the flesh. They leave families, children, husbands and wives and do it "in the name of the Lord." This is ridiculous and deceptive. God will never destroy your marriage or your home. It is not the will of God. He is a God who heals, restores, and mends. The emphasis I place here is total obedience to the calling of God, *whatever the cost.*

Your Assignment May Require You To Walk Away From Something Important To You.

"What You Can Walk Away From You Have Mastered — What You Can't Walk Away From Has Mastered You."

-Mike Murdock-

⟶ 25 ⟵

WHAT YOU ARE WILLING TO WALK AWAY FROM DETERMINES WHAT GOD WILL BRING TO YOU.

Your future is much greater than your present.

You simply must be willing to walk away from your present. God has plans. He has bigger plans than your imagination could ever create for a lifetime.

If you are willing to walk away from something important to you, God will compensate you over and over again.

If you fail to walk away, the consequences and the disasters are also inevitable.

Three Tragic Examples Of Those Who Refused To Walk Away

Samson refused to walk away from Delilah. He became a joke and a sport to the Philistines. His eyes were gouged out. His days of championship were over.

Judas refused to walk away from thirty pieces of silver. He committed suicide. His name will never be recorded in the Heroes' Hall of Faith.

Demas would not walk away from the magnetism of the world. He became a mere footnote in the writings of Paul. "For Demas hath forsaken me, having loved this present world, and is departed" (2 Timothy 4:10).

Three Champions Who Were Willing To Walk Away

Moses was willing to walk away from the palace of Pharaoh. He esteemed the reproach of Christ to be greater than the treasures of Egypt. The favor of God surrounded him and hundreds of years after his death, he is mentioned as one of the Heroes of Faith in Hebrews 11. "By faith Moses, when he was come to years, refused to be called the son of Pharaoh's daughter; Choosing rather to suffer affliction with the people of God, than to enjoy the pleasures of sin for a season; Esteeming the reproach of Christ greater riches than the treasures in Egypt: for he had respect unto the recompense of the reward. By faith he forsook Egypt, not fearing the wrath of the king: for he endured, as seeing Him who is invisible" (Hebrews 11:24-27).

Joseph was willing to walk away from the temptation of Potiphar's wife. God gave him the throne. He became Prime Minister and one of the most revered men of God in the entire Bible.

Ruth was willing to walk away from Moab. She met a remarkable, wealthy and godly man named Boaz. They produced a son, Obed, who produced Jesse. Jesse, the father of David and grandfather of Solomon, ushered in the lineage of Jesus of Nazareth.

What You Are Willing To Walk Away From

Determines Who God Will Bring Into Your Life As Well.

Are you single? I have been single for many years. In my early years of singleness, loneliness was often overpowering. I became militant, argumentative and agitated with God. I wanted to hold on to relationships that helped to distract me from the pain and emptiness of aloneness. But, God reminded me of this powerful principle: What You Are Willing To Walk Away From Determines What He Will Bring To You.

Five Rules For Relationships

1. Never Stay *Where* You Have Not Been Assigned.
2. Never Stay Around *Someone* Who Is Not Assigned To You.
3. Never Stay Where You Are Not *Celebrated.*
4. Never Stay In A Relationship That Feeds Your *Weakness,* Instead Of Your Strength.
5. Never Stay In A Relationship That *Keeps* You In Your *Present,* Instead Of *Moving* You Toward Your *Future.*

It is often difficult to end a comfortable relationship. It is difficult to walk away from a relationship that eases the loneliness, the inner vacuum that distracts you from your solitary times. But often, when God gives you an Assignment, He will require you to give up a relationship that really matters to you.

That is why Jesus hastened to reassure Peter that any losses would be *recognized and restored* if total obedience occurred. "Then Peter began to say unto Him, Lo, we have left all, and have followed

Thee. And Jesus answered and said, Verily I say unto you, There is no man that hath left house, or brethren, or sisters, or father, or mother, or wife, or children, or lands, for My sake, and the gospel's, But he shall receive an hundredfold now in this time, houses, and brethren, and sisters, and mothers, and children, and lands, with persecutions; and in the world to come eternal life" (Mark 10:28-30).

God may require you to temporarily walk away from financial security. The widow of Zarephath had to walk away from her last meal. She was starving. The famine was everywhere. Elijah showed up at her door with a request. "And Elijah said unto her, Fear not; go and do as thou hast said: but make me thereof a little cake first, and bring it unto me, and after make for thee and for thy son" (1 Kings 17:13).

What a rare and difficult decision she was forced to make! Her son was dying. He was emaciated, weakened and almost dead. It was to be their last meal together. A man of God instructed her to *walk away* from her own provision, her last meal on earth. People sometimes criticize ministers who ask for donations to their vision. They sneer and make snide remarks about a man of God who strongly urges them to sow their Seed into the soil of lost souls. Television commentators often target ministers who emphasize finances in any way. Yet, Elijah instructed a woman to *walk away* from her Seed, *her last meal.*

She obeyed.

Her *future* was more important than her *present.*

Her *Seed* was more important than her *meal.*

His *word* was more important than her *pain.*

The prophet explained the Principle of Increase:

"For thus saith the Lord God of Israel, The barrel of meal shall not waste, neither shall the cruse of oil fail, until the day that the Lord sendeth rain upon the earth. And she went and did according to the saying of Elijah: and she, and he, and her house, did eat many days. And the barrel of meal wasted not, neither did the cruse of oil fail, according to the word of the Lord, which he spake by Elijah" (1 Kings 17:14-16).

Here is her incentive for obedience: *provision*.

What You Are Willing To Walk Away From Determines What God Will Bring To You.

An incredible experience happened in my life several years ago.

I had just received a royalty check for more than $8,500 from my song writing. I was ecstatic. I had just completed three crusades in Poland, East Africa, and Brazil. I had arrived home, and went straight to preach for a minister friend of mine, Rod Parsley in Columbus, Ohio. At the conclusion of the service, I turned the service to Pastor Parsley to receive an offering for my ministry. Just as I was about to hand the microphone to him, the Holy Spirit instructed me to receive a special offering for the pastor instead of my own ministry. I have always been swift to obey the Lord, so I proceeded.

Suddenly, while I was explaining to the people that there would be no offering received for me at all, we would give one to the pastor and his wife instead, the Holy Spirit spoke. It was not a command. It was not really an instruction. It was more like a suggestion. It seemed like an *invitation to an investment*. I had never had such an experience before.

"How would you like to explore and experiment with what I could do with your $8,500?"

I froze. This $8,500 was my *Harvest*. I was thrilled. I had great plans how to spend it. It was going to be *fun* money. He spoke again in the form of a question.

"How would you like to *explore and experiment* with what I could do with your $8,500?"

I knew His voice. I was in His presence. I have spent many years preaching this gospel around the world. He was giving me an opportunity to prove His power, His love and His creativity in my life. I thought for several minutes. Actually, I thought for about 45 minutes. What could I do with $8,500? *That was a lot of money!* But, I kept thinking. I could buy a small car, fly to Europe and live for about thirty days or I could put a down payment on a small rent house somewhere.

I thought a second time. *What could He do with my $8,500?* I remembered the five loaves and two fishes of the little boy. Jesus used them to feed the multitude. As long as the little boy was holding the five loaves and two fishes, it remained just five loaves and two fishes. It dawned on me...

Nothing Multiplies Until It Is In The Hands Of Jesus. It is always His touch that brings the multiplication.

If I *kept* the $8,500, $8,500 is the *most* it would ever be.

If I sowed the $8,500, $8,500 is the *least* it would ever be.

Then, I asked myself another question. Is $8,500 all I will ever need *the rest of my life*? Is that enough money to do my entire future vision and goals and dreams? Of course not. I had to realize it myself. One car alone would cost much more than $8,500. A new home would cost many times more than that amount. Something within me rose up strongly to believe God. I chose to believe that He wanted to *bless* me.

▶ I chose to believe my future could be *unlike my present.*

▶ I chose to *honor* the inner whisperings of the Holy Spirit.

▶ I chose to *use my faith* at one of the highest levels in my lifetime.

I planted the entire $8,500 as a Seed of Faith.

When I walked into my hotel room that night, I plummeted into an unexplainable depression. I could hardly speak for seven days. Satan worked on my mind. He continuously sneered and laughed and said to me, "That was not the Holy Spirit at all. That was your imagination that told you to plant the $8,500. It was not God. You will never see any results to this Seed. You have just lost $8,500."

I felt sick inside. I really believed him. I felt stupid. I felt ignorant. I felt like I had been taken in by my own weakness and sowed a Seed that was unnecessary in response to an imagination of my own mind.

About seven days later, I cried out to God in my Secret Place. "I sowed this Seed of $8,500 in an attempt to obey you. If I missed Your will, I am sorry, but I did it in an attempt to please You."

He spoke only one sentence back to my heart but I have never forgotten that sentence: "Anything you do in an attempt to please Me, will not go unrewarded."

Anything You Do In An Attempt To Please God Will Not Go Unrewarded.

Six weeks later, I was staying at the Hyatt Regency Hotel in Houston, Texas. I arose at 5:30 a.m. for my prayer time. At 7:15 a.m., the Holy Spirit suddenly gave me an idea. It was to take 2,000 Scriptures and place them in categories for businessmen. I decided to call it, "The Businessman's Topical Bible." It would make it possible for any Christian businessman to find a Scripture within ten seconds concerning any difficult season he was experiencing in business.

Then, I saw a photograph in my heart of "The Mother's Topical Bible." It would help mothers to find Scriptures by categories, depending on the difficulty they were going through with their husbands or children. The same picture came to me for "The Father's Topical Bible." Then, I saw another one in my heart—"The Teenager's Topical Bible."

I telephoned a publisher. They agreed to pay me a royalty from each Bible printed. They promised to place the Bibles in 1,300 bookstores across the United States on a regular basis. They would give me a royalty percentage of every one that sold for the remaining of the contract as long as I wanted it.

God has since blessed those Topical Bibles beyond my imagination. To date, over 600,000 have been sold!

In fact, when a major Christian booksellers' association chose the top one hundred reference books in the United States, five of the first twenty were my topical Bibles! I was able to buy my mother and father cars, renovate their home, and help put young preachers through Bible college. Every ninety days, I still receive a royalty check.

I was willing to walk away from the $8,500.

God has rewarded me many, many times over.

Your Willingness To Walk Away From Your Present Is Your Greatest Qualification For Your Future.

I shared this in Florida some months ago. A woman approached me and asked me to anoint her special Seed for $8,500. She had heard me say that God had given me a *lifetime income from a one-time Seed.* She wanted to experience the same miracle by planting a Lifetime Blessing Seed of $8,500.

I agreed to covenant with her that God would do for her exactly what He had done for me. Within months, she settled a lawsuit. Her reward? More than $400,000.

What You Are Willing To Walk Away From Determines What God Will Bring To You.

God may be speaking to you this very moment. He may be talking to you about planting a significant and powerful Seed into His work. It keeps arising in your mind. It stays in your heart. Yet, your own bills and needs appear overpowering. You are facing a mountain of debt. You are hesitant, even fearful. Let me encourage you today to embrace the words of God to you.

God will never lie to you. "God is not a man, that He should lie; neither the son of man, that He should repent: hath He said, and shall He not do it? or hath He spoken, and shall He not make it good?" (Numbers 23:19).

What You Are Willing To Walk Away From Determines What God Will Bring To You.

"Broken People Become Masters At Mending."

- Mike Murdock -

⇔ 26 ⇔

IT IS POSSIBLE TO BE RESTORED AFTER YOU HAVE MADE A MAJOR MISTAKE IN YOUR ASSIGNMENT.

━━━━━━⇒⊱•◦•⊰⇐━━━━━━

Mistakes are Gates.

A mistake is not a conclusion. A mistake is an entry into another season.

14 Facts You Should Know About Your Mistakes

1. *Recognize That God Anticipates Your Mistakes.* "For He knoweth our frame; He remembereth that we are dust...But the mercy of the Lord is from everlasting to everlasting upon them that fear Him, and His righteousness unto children's children" (Psalm 103:14,17).

2. *When You Make A Mistake, Have An Immediate Conference With God.* "Come now, and let us reason together, saith the Lord: though your sins be as scarlet, they shall be as white as snow; though they be red like crimson, they shall be as wool" (Isaiah 1:18).

3. *Remember, No Mistake Is Too Big To Be Forgiven.* Listen to Paul. "This *is* a faithful saying, and worthy of all acceptation, that Christ Jesus came into the world to save sinners; of whom I am chief. Howbeit for this cause I obtained mercy, that in me first Jesus Christ might shew forth all longsuffering, for a pattern to them which should hereafter believe on Him to life everlasting" (1 Timothy 1:15,16).

4. *Believe That Mistakes Will Never Erase The Love Of Christ Toward You.* "Who shall separate us from the love of Christ? shall tribulation, or distress, or persecution, or famine, or nakedness, or peril, or sword? As it is written, For Thy sake we are killed all the day long; we are accounted as sheep for the slaughter. Nay, in all these things we are more than conquerors through Him that loved us. For I am persuaded, that neither death, nor life, nor angels, nor principalities, nor powers, nor things present, nor things to come, Nor height, nor depth, nor any other creature, shall be able to separate us from the love of God, which is in Christ Jesus our Lord" (Romans 8:35-39).

5. *Look For The Plans Of God On The Other Side Of Your Mistakes.* Why does He endure and show longsuffering to us? "And that He might make known the riches of His glory on the vessels of mercy" (Romans 9:23).

6. *Expect Your Tragedies To Become Your Trophies.* David is an eternal Trophy on display in the Museum of Miracles. Carefully listen to his heart's cry after adultery with Bathsheba and having her husband, Uriah, murdered on the field of battle. "Wash me throughly from mine iniquity, and cleanse

me from my sin. For I acknowledge my transgressions: and my sin is ever before me...Purge me with hyssop, and I shall be clean: wash me, and I shall be whiter than snow. Make me to hear joy and gladness; that the bones which Thou hast broken may rejoice. Hide Thy face from my sins, and blot out all mine iniquities. Create in me a clean heart, O God; and renew a right spirit within me. Cast me not away from Thy presence; and take not Thy Holy Spirit from me. Restore unto me the joy of thy salvation; and uphold me with Thy free spirit" (Psalm 51:2,7-12).

7. *Hate The Mistake Enough To Repent And Turn From It.* "But shewed first unto them of Damascus, and at Jerusalem, and throughout all the coasts of Judaea, and then to the Gentiles, that they should repent and turn to God, and do works meet for repentance" (Acts 26:20).

8. *Acknowledge Your Transgression And Ask For Restoration.* "Ask, and it shall be given you; seek, and ye shall find; knock, and it shall be opened unto you: For every one that asketh receiveth; and he that seeketh findeth; and to him that knocketh it shall be opened" (Matthew 7:7,8).

9. *Recognize That Your Heavenly Father Is The Only One Who Can Make You Clean Again.* Your personal works, resolutions, and vows will not restore you. "For by grace are ye saved through faith; and that not of yourselves: it is the gift of God: Not of works, lest any man should boast" (Ephesians 2:8,9). Any damaged product must be returned to the manufacturer for repairs.

10. *Confess Mistakes To Those In Spiritual*

Authority Over Your Life Who Can Pray A Prayer Of Deliverance. "Confess your faults one to another, and pray one for another, that ye may be healed. The effectual fervent prayer of a righteous man availeth much" (James 5:16).

11. *Pursue And Permit Restoration By Those Who Love You.* "Brethren, if a man be overtaken in a fault, ye which are spiritual, restore such an one in the spirit of meekness; considering thyself, lest thou also be tempted" (Galatians 6:1).

12. *Restore Anything You Have Wrongly Taken From Another.* Zacchaeus understood this principle. "And Zacchaeus stood, and said unto the Lord; Behold, Lord, the half of my goods I give to the poor; and if I have taken any thing from any man by false accusation, I restore him fourfold" (Luke 19:8).

13. *Focus On Your Future Instead Of Your Failure.* "Remember ye not the former things, neither consider the things of old. Behold, I will do a new thing: now it shall spring forth; shall ye not know it? I will even make a way in the wilderness, and rivers in the desert" (Isaiah 43:18,19).

14. *Teach Others The Laws Of Restoration.* David declared that when God restored him, he would teach others the laws of restoration. "Then will I teach transgressors thy ways; and sinners shall be converted unto thee" (Psalm 51:13).

Would you take a moment to pray this brief prayer with me today? Will you pray this sincerely from the depths of your heart?

"Heavenly Father,

I know I have sinned.

I hate the mistakes in my life.

Somehow, You have given me another day to pursue You and begin changes.

I cannot do it alone.

You alone can change my heart, my desires and my destiny.

I choose to believe that Your *mercy* is more powerful than my *mistakes*.

Your love is more powerful than my losses.

Your *power* is stronger than my *pain*.

Your *Wisdom* can mend my weakness.

You are my God.

I am Your child.

Begin the changes in me today.

Forgive me of every sin: as I submit totally to Your authority and life today.

I believe that Your blood cleanses and purifies every stain on my conscience, my memories, and my life.

From this moment forward, I will follow You as Savior, Lord, and Master of my life.

In Jesus' name, confirm Your presence by Your instant peace and overwhelming joy this very moment. Amen and Amen."

Now, rise up again! And remember, permit those closest to you to receive *that same mercy*.

Broken People Become Masters At Mending.

Begin to mend those around you this very day.

It Is Possible To Be Restored After You Have Made A Major Mistake In Your Assignment.

**"All Men Fail, The Great Ones
Get Back Up."**

- Mike Murdock -

≈ 27 ≈

THE BIBLE REVEALS THE RECOVERY SYSTEM FOR ANYONE WHO FAILS IN THEIR ASSIGNMENT.

Everybody falls.
Champions get back up.
Study the life of Peter. It is always wise to attend the Personal Workshop of Peter, when he teaches on "The Laws of Restoration." He tasted personal failure. When he denied the Lord three times, the sudden realization of his weakness was overwhelming. "And he went out, and wept bitterly" (Matthew 26:75). Nobody will ever know the emotional havoc Peter experienced in his heart and soul. It is quite possible that he considered suicide like Judas. It is likely that he felt unwanted, undesirable and unnecessary.

But, somewhere in his relationship with Jesus, he caught a glimpse of mercy. *He had studied love with the Master of Love.* He had studied The Laws of Restoration from the One who restored thousands in a moment. He had watched Jesus look up into a tree, then have supper with a deceptive tax collector. He had memories of the demon possessed being set free by their deliverer.

Oh, you and I serve a second-chance God! I wrote a wonderful song several years ago called, "He's Done it Once, He's Done it Twice and He Can Do it Again."

He's done it once.
He's done it twice.
And, He can do it again.
He's done it once.
He's done it twice.
And, He can do it again.

Every miracle that I need.
Every miracle that I need.

He's done it once.
He's done it twice.
And, He can do it again.

⸻

Study the life of Samson.

Samson is remembered on *earth* for Delilah.

Samson is remembered in *heaven* for his *recovery.*

After his eyes were gouged out, God used him even in his death to kill the enemies of God. "So the dead which he slew in his death were more than they which he slew in his life" (Judges 16:30).

Samson recovered from the shame, the humiliation and embarrassment. In fact, hundreds of years after his death, the writer of the Book of Hebrews included him in the same chapter with

Abraham, Moses, Joseph and David.

Study the life of Paul.

Look at this great Apostle. He was a hater, a persecutor of Christians. His name had been Saul. Those who stoned Stephen laid their clothes at his feet. "As for Saul, he made havock of the church, entering into every house, and haling men and women committed them to prison" (Acts 8:3). But, God turned him around.

Is it possible for someone to really change? Ask the Apostle Paul. "And I thank Christ Jesus our Lord, who hath enabled me, for that he counted me faithful, putting me into the ministry; Who was before a blasphemer, and a persecutor, and injurious: but I obtained mercy, because I did it ignorantly in unbelief. And the grace of our Lord was exceeding abundant with faith and love which is in Christ Jesus" (1 Timothy 1:12-14).

If You Fail During Your Assignment, Pursue The Counsel Of Champions Who Got Back Up.

The Bible Reveals The Recovery System For Anyone Who Fails In Their Assignment.

"Your Uniqueness/Distinction Is Not In
Your Similarity To Another, But In
Your Difference From Others."

Mike Murdock

～ 28 ～

GOD IS LOOKING AT SOMETHING IN YOU OTHERS CANNOT SEE.

Something incredible is inside you.

Your Assignment was decided in your mother's womb. "Before I formed thee in the belly I knew thee; and before thou camest forth out of the womb I sanctified thee, and I ordained thee a prophet unto the nations" (Jeremiah 1:5). God knows it. He created you. He has known the invisible purpose for which you were created.

You are not an accident waiting to happen. "I will praise Thee; for I am fearfully and wonderfully made: marvellous are Thy works; and that my soul knoweth right well" (Psalm 139:14).

Everything inside you is known, treasured and intended for full use by your Creator. "My substance was not hid from Thee, when I was made in secret, and curiously wrought in the lowest parts of the earth" (Psalm 139:15).

Your flaws do not necessarily prevent God from using you. They exist to motivate your pursuit of Him. "Thine eyes did see my substance, yet being unperfect; and in Thy book all my members were written, which in continuance were fashioned, when as yet there was none of them" (Psalm 139:16).

Your very existence excites God. "How precious also are Thy thoughts unto me, O God! how great is the sum of them! If I should count them, they are more in number than the sand: when I awake, I am still with Thee" (Psalm 139:17,18).

Picture an author exultant over his book. The book exists. The author created it. He is excited about it, whether anyone else is or not. Imagine a composer, exhilarated over a completed song. He knew its beginning and its ending. Its very presence excites him.

Your very presence energizes God. He saw your beginning and the desired conclusion. "For Thou hast created all things, and for Thy pleasure they are and were created" (Revelation 4:11).

God is looking at something within you *that you have never seen.* "For man looketh on the outward appearance, but the Lord looketh on the heart" (1 Samuel 16:7).

God is looking at something inside you *satan cannot even discern.* "Lest Satan should get an advantage of us: for we are ignorant of his devices" (2 Corinthians 2:11).

God is looking at something you contain that *you have not yet discovered.* "For as the heavens are higher than the earth, so are My ways higher than your ways, and My thoughts than your thoughts" (Isaiah 55:9).

God will tell you secrets satan will never hear.

His mercies are not wasted on you. He has big plans. His forgiveness is not futile. You are *becoming* a monument and trophy of His grace. "For we are

His workmanship, created in Christ Jesus unto good works" (Ephesians 2:10).

God boasts about you to every demon. (See Job 1:8.)

You may be looking at your *beginning.*
God is looking at your *end.*
You may be obsessed with your *flaws.*
God is obsessed with your *future.*
You may be focusing on your *enemies.*
God is focusing on your *eventuality.*

God is not *awaiting* your becoming. He is awaiting your *discovery* of it.

So never consult those who have not discovered what is within you. Their focus is different. Their conclusions are inaccurate.

Stay in the presence of the One Who created you. You will always feel confident about yourself when you stay in His presence. He is looking at something in you that is remarkable. He planted it within you while you were yet in your mother's womb.

David understood this. King Saul and his brothers saw brashness; the Holy Spirit saw *boldness.* His brothers saw anger; God saw a sense of *justice.*

Joseph understood this. His brothers saw pride. God saw *thankfulness.* The brothers saw rivalry; God saw a *weapon.*

That's why the opinions and observations of others are not your foundation for greatness. Stop pursuing their conclusions. God is looking at something inside you they *cannot see, refuse* to see and may never see.

The brothers of Jesus did not grasp His *divinity.*

The brothers of Joseph *misinterpreted him.*

The brothers of David saw a mere shepherd boy.

The friends of Job could not discern the satanic scenario *before his crisis.*

Haman could not even discern the nationality of Esther!

Few are ever accurate in their assessment of you. *Few.*

Your flaws are *much less* than they imagine.

Your greatness is far greater than they discern.

The Holy Spirit is the only One who has accurately assessed your *future,* your *ingredients* and the *willingness* of your heart to become great. That's why He keeps reaching, pursuing and developing you in the midst of every attack and crisis.

He never *gives up* on you.

He never *quits looking at you.*

He never *changes His plans* toward you.

He never quits believing in your future.

He has decided the conclusion and is only awaiting your discovery of it.

Remember this continuously. God is seeing something inside you that keeps Him excited and involved. "Then Samuel took the horn of oil, and anointed him in the midst of his brethren: and the Spirit of the Lord came upon David from that day forward" (1 Samuel 16:13).

God Is Looking At Something In You Others Cannot See.

≈ 29 ≈

THE SUCCESS OF YOUR ASSIGNMENT IS HIDDEN IN YOUR DAILY ROUTINE.

Your daily habits create your future.

What you do daily determines, what you become permanently. Habit will always take you further than desire.

Creating a perfect day is a vital discovery. Duplicating that kind of day consistently will guarantee uncommon success. Here are seven keys to creating a perfect day in your life.

Seven Ingredients Of A Perfect Day

1. *You Must Make Significant And Measurable Movement Toward Good Health.* "What? know ye not that your body is the temple of the Holy Ghost which is in you, which ye have of God, and ye are not your own? For ye are bought with a price: therefore glorify God in your body, and in your spirit, which are God's" (1 Corinthians 6:19,20).

2. *You Must Make Measurable And Significant Movement Toward Order.* Order is the accurate arrangement of things. I have noticed that the smallest effort in drawing up a plan for the day, cleaning out my closet, or rearrangement of books

in my library, generates joy. The slightest movement toward order generates a measure of pleasure. "But as God hath distributed to every man, as the Lord hath called every one, so let him walk" (1 Corinthians 7:17).

3. *You Must Make Measurable And Significant Movement Toward Uncommon Wisdom.* "Wisdom is the principal thing" (Proverbs 4:7).

4. *You Must Make Measurable And Significant Movement Toward Financial Stability.* "Beloved I wish above all things that thou mayest prosper and be in health, even as thy soul prospereth" (3 John 1:2).

5. *You Must Make Measurable And Significant Movement Toward Your Assignment.* "Whatsoever thy hand findeth to do, do it with thy might" (Ecclesiastes 9:10).

6. *You Must Nurture And Develop Significant Relationships.* You must monitor, motivate, and mentor those who are in your Love Circle. "Two are better than one; because they have a good reward for their labour. For if they fall, the one will lift up his fellow: but woe to him that is alone when he falleth; for he hath not another to help him up. And if one prevail against him, two shall withstand him; and a threefold cord is not quickly broken" (Ecclesiastes 4:9,10,12).

7. *You Must Listen Constantly To The Voice Of The Holy Spirit.* He is your lifetime companion. "And I will pray the Father, and He shall give you another Comforter, that He may abide with you for ever; Even the Spirit of truth; Whom the world cannot receive, because it seeth Him not, neither

knoweth Him: but ye know Him; for He dwelleth with you, and shall be in you" (John 14:16,17).

Your Assignment is a *daily* miracle.

It is a *daily* event.

You are only responsible for *today.*

When you learn how to obey the voice of the Holy Spirit *hourly,* you will have learned the secret of life.

The Success Of Your Assignment Is Hidden In Your Daily Routine.

"Knowing Who You Are Not Assigned To Is As Important As Knowing To Whom You Are Assigned."

Mike Murdock

~ 30 ~

YOUR GREATEST PAIN SOMETIMES COMES FROM THOSE TO WHOM YOU ARE ASSIGNED.

It is inevitable.

The servant is not greater than his lord.

Jesus Himself experienced this pain. "O Jerusalem, Jerusalem, thou that killest the prophets, and stonest them which are sent unto thee, how often would I have gathered thy children together, even as a hen gathereth her chickens under her wings, and ye would not!" (Matthew 23:37).

It happened to our precious Savior. And, it will happen to you as well.

Every mother has already experienced this pain. She has known the torment and the toil of a child within her womb for nine months. Then, to watch that child grow up and scream and throw temper tantrums and cry out, "I cannot wait to get away from this house! I hate you!" Every father has known this kind of pain as well.

The comments of neighbors do not necessarily break the heart of parents. It's the comments of the children.

Every pastor knows this pain. He has labored, studied and interceded for his congregation. He has spent hours of counseling and orchestrating the greatest gathering of speakers and others who could minister to his people—only to find out that the family he invested the most time in, has decided to go across town to another church "where they can get their soul fed."

The psalmist knew this pain. "Yea, mine own familiar friend, in whom I trusted, which did eat of my bread, hath lifted up his heel against me" (Psalm 41:9).

Don't be demoralized by the unexpected pain or warfare. It is normal to every warrior.

It is the Father's secret for feeding your addiction to Him and His presence.

Your Greatest Pain Sometimes Comes From Those To Whom You Are Assigned.

~ 31 ~

YOUR ASSIGNMENT WILL REQUIRE THE NATURE, SKILLS AND MENTALITY OF A WARRIOR.

Your Assignment will move from battle to battle.
Adversity is inevitable. Your enemy observes all progress. God will mentor you in warfare. "He teacheth my hands to war, so that a bow of steel is broken by mine arms" (Psalm 18:34). "Blessed be the Lord my strength, which teacheth my hands to war, and my fingers to fight" (Psalm 144:1).

18 Qualities Of The Uncommon Warrior

1. *The Uncommon Warrior Only Uses The Weapons That Have Never Failed Him.* He does not use the weapons of others. David used the weapon he was most familiar with—his sling. (See 1 Samuel 17:38-40).

2. *The Uncommon Warrior Refuses To Use The Armor And Weaponry Of Others Who Had Failed Before Him.* David did. "And Saul armed David with his armour, and he put an helmet of brass upon his head; also he armed him with a coat of mail. And David girded his sword upon his armour, and

he assayed to go; for he had not proved it. And David said unto Saul, I cannot go with these; for I have not proved them. And David put them off him" (1 Samuel 17:38,39).

3. *The Uncommon Warrior Knows He Has Something His Enemy Fears.* David had a willingness to fight. "And David said to Saul, Let no man's heart fail because of him; thy servant will go and fight with this Philistine" (1 Samuel 17:32).

4. *The Uncommon Warrior Knows The True Source Of His Competence And Confidence.* David did. "David said moreover, The Lord that delivered me out of the paw of the lion, and out of the paw of the bear, He will deliver me out of the hand of this Philistine" (1 Samuel 17:37).

5. *The Uncommon Warrior Knows That The Power Of God Is Greater Than The Weapons Of Man.* David did. "Then said David to the Philistine, Thou comest to me with a sword, and with a spear, and with a shield: but I come to thee in the name of the Lord of hosts, the God of the armies of Israel, Whom thou has defied" (1 Samuel 17:45).

6. *The Uncommon Warrior Often Uses, In His Greatest Battles, The Skills Developed In His Daily Routine.* David did. "And he took his staff in his hand, and chose him five smooth stones out of the brook, and put them in a shepherd's bag which he had, even in a scrip; and his sling was in his hand: and he drew near to the Philistine" (1 Samuel 17:40).

7. *The Uncommon Warrior Expects To Be An Instrument In The Hand Of God To Destroy His Enemy.* David did. He said "and I will smite thee, and take thine head from thee; and I will give the

carcases of the host of the Philistines this day unto the fowls of the air, and to the wild beasts of the earth; that all the earth may know that there is a God in Israel" (1 Samuel 17:46).

8.   *The Uncommon Warrior Expects His Enemies To Fall And He Publicly Predicts His Victory.* David did. "This day will the Lord deliver thee into mine hand" (1 Samuel 17:46). "When mine enemies are turned back, they shall fall and perish at Thy presence. For Thou hast maintained my right and my cause; Thou satest in the throne judging right. Thou hast rebuked the heathen, Thou has destroyed the wicked, Thou hast put out their name for ever and ever...But the Lord shall endure for ever" (Psalm 9:3-5,7).

9.   *The Uncommon Warrior Stays On The Offensive Running Toward His Enemy.* David did. "And it came to pass, when the Philistine arose, and came and drew nigh to meet David, that David hasted, and ran toward the army to meet the Philistine" (1 Samuel 17:48).

10.   *The Uncommon Warrior Expects The Spectators Of The Battle To Observe And Experience The Power Of God.* David did. "And all this assembly shall know that the Lord saveth not with sword and spear: for the battle is the Lord's, and He will give you into our hands" (1 Samuel 17:47).

11.   *The Uncommon Warrior Keeps Vibrant Memories Of Past Victories.* David did. "And David said unto Saul, The servant kept his father's sheep, and there came a lion, and a bear, and took a lamb out of the flock: And I went out after him, and smote him, and delivered it out of his mouth: and when he arose against me, I caught him by his beard, and

smote him, and slew him. Thy servant slew both the lion and the bear: and this uncircumcised Philistine shall be as one of them, seeing he hath defied the armies of the living God" (1 Samuel 17:34-36).

12. *The Uncommon Warrior Ignores The Opinions Of Obvious Losers And Failures Around Him.* David did. "And Eliab his eldest brother heard when he spake unto the men; and Eliab's anger was kindled against David, and he said, Why camest thou down hither? and with whom hast thou left those few sheep in the wilderness? I know thy pride, and the naughtiness of thine heart; for thou art come down that thou mightest see the battle. And David said, What have I now done? Is there not a cause? And he turned from him toward another, and spake after the same manner: and the people answered him again after the former manner" (1 Samuel 17:28-30).

13. *The Uncommon Warrior Pursues, Savors And Celebrates The Rewards Of Every Victory.* David did. "And David spake to the men that stood by him, saying, What shall be done to the man that killeth this Philistine, and taketh away the reproach from Israel? for who is this uncircumcised Philistine, that he should defy the armies of the living God?...it shall be, that the man who killeth him, the king will enrich him with great riches, and will give him his daughter, and make his father's house free in Israel" (1 Samuel 17:26,25).

14. *The Uncommon Warrior Keeps His Promise To Destroy His Enemy.* David did. "Therefore David ran, and stood upon the Philistine, and took his sword, and drew it out of the sheath thereof, and

slew him, and cut off his head therewith" (1 Samuel 17:51).

15. *The Uncommon Warrior Unashamedly Displays The Spoils Of Past Victories As Trophies Of Thanksgiving.* David even carried the head of Goliath around with him. "And as David returned from the slaughter of the Philistine, Abner took him, and brought him before Saul with the head of the Philistine in his hand" (1 Samuel 17:57).

16. *The Uncommon Warrior Creates His Own Museum Of Memories To Celebrate His Victories.* David did. "And David took the head of the Philistine, and brought it to Jerusalem; but he put his armour in his tent" (1 Samuel 17:54).

17. *The Uncommon Warrior Knows That The Defeat Of His Strongest Adversary Will Cause His Other Enemies To Flee.* David saw this. When Goliath fell, his followers fled. "And when the Philistines saw their champion was dead, they fled" (1 Samuel 17:51).

18. *The Uncommon Warrior Knows That When He Is Victorious, The Discouraged Around Him Become Encouraged And Energized.* David saw this happen. "And the men of Israel and of Judah arose, and shouted, and pursued the Philistines, until thou come to the valley, and to the gates of Ekron. And the wounded of the Philistines fell down by the way to Shaaraim, even unto Gath, and unto Ekron" (1 Samuel 17:52).

Somebody else needs to see you win.

Preparation is the key to successful warfare.

Your Assignment Will Require The Nature, Skills And Mentality Of A Warrior.

DECISION!

Will You Accept Jesus As Savior Of Your Life Today?

The Bible says, "That if thou shalt confess with thy mouth the Lord Jesus, and shall believe in thine heart that God hath raised Him from the dead, thou shalt be saved. For with the heart man believeth unto righteousness; and with the mouth confession is made unto salvation." (Romans 10:9-10)

To receive Jesus Christ as Lord and Savior of your life, please pray this prayer from your heart today!

"Dear Jesus, I believe that You died for me and rose again on the third day. I confess I am a sinner. I need Your love and forgiveness. Come into my life, forgive my sins, and give me eternal life. I confess You now as my Lord. Thank You for my salvation, Your peace and joy. Amen."

FREE!
My Best-Selling Book
"101 Wisdom Keys"

You can receive today your personal gift copy of this life-changing book. Contained inside this volume are some of the most powerful Wisdom Keys God has ever imparted to my heart. Make this book your personal Wisdom guide. Keep it handy. Apply the principles. Your life will be transformed forever! It is my Seed of Blessing into every friend who pursues the Wisdom of God.

Order Today!
Call 940-891-1400
for your free copy
(during normal business hours)

❑ Yes, Mike! I made a decision to accept Christ as my personal Savior today. Please send me my free gift of your book *"31 Keys to a New Beginning"* to help me with my new life in Christ. *(B48)*

❑ Yes, Mike, please rush my personal free copy of your powerful book *"101 Wisdom Keys."* (A $7 value.) *Extra copies are only $7 each. (B45)*

Please Print

NAME

ADDRESS

CITY   STATE   ZIP

PHONE   BIRTHDAY

Mail Form to: Dr. Mike Murdock • P. O. Box 99 • Denton, TX 76202

Clip and Mail

251

ORDER FORM The Mike Murdock Wisdom Library

(All books paperback unless indicated otherwise.)

Qty	Code	Book Title	USA	Total
	B01	Wisdom For Winning	$10	
	B02	5 Steps Out Of Depression	$ 3	
	B03	The Sex Trap	$ 3	
	B04	10 Lies People Believe About Money	$ 3	
	B05	Finding Your Purpose In Life	$ 3	
	B06	Creating Tomorrow Through Seed-Faith	$ 3	
	B07	Battle Techniques For War Weary Saints	$ 3	
	B08	Enjoying The Winning Life	$ 3	
	B09	Four Forces/Guarantee Career Success	$ 3	
	B10	The Bridge Called Divorce	$ 3	
	B11	Dream Seeds	$ 9	
	B12	Young Ministers Handbook	$20	
	B13	Seeds Of Wisdom On Dreams And Goals	$ 3	
	B14	Seeds Of Wisdom On Relationships	$ 3	
	B15	Seeds Of Wisdom On Miracles	$ 3	
	B16	Seeds Of Wisdom On Seed-Faith	$ 3	
	B17	Seeds Of Wisdom On Overcoming	$ 3	
	B18	Seeds Of Wisdom On Habits	$ 3	
	B19	Seeds Of Wisdom On Warfare	$ 3	
	B20	Seeds Of Wisdom On Obedience	$ 3	
	B21	Seeds Of Wisdom On Adversity	$ 3	
	B22	Seeds Of Wisdom On Prosperity	$ 3	
	B23	Seeds Of Wisdom On Prayer	$ 3	
	B24	Seeds Of Wisdom On Faith-Talk	$ 3	
	B25	Seeds Of Wisdom One Year Devotional	$10	
	B26	The God Book	$10	
	B27	The Jesus Book	$10	
	B28	The Blessing Bible	$10	
	B29	The Survival Bible	$10	
	B30	The Teen's Topical Bible	$ 6	
	B30L	The Teen's Topical Bible (Leather)	$20	
	B31	The One-Minute Topical Bible	$10	
	B32	The Minister's Topical Bible	$ 6	
	B33	The Businessman's Topical Bible	$ 6	
	B33L	The Businessman's Topical Bible (Leather)	$20	
	B34L	The Grandparent's Topical Bible (Leather)	$20	
	B35	The Father's Topical Bible	$ 6	
	B35L	The Father's Topical Bible (Leather)	$20	
	B36	The Mother's Topical Bible	$ 6	
	B36L	The Mother's Topical Bible (Leather)	$20	
	B37	The New Convert's Topical Bible	$15	
	B38	The Widow's Topical Bible	$ 6	
	B39	The Double Diamond Principle	$ 9	
	B40	Wisdom For Crisis Times	$ 9	
	B41	The Gift Of Wisdom (Volume One)	$ 8	
	B42	One-Minute Businessman's Devotional	$10	
	B43	One-Minute Businesswoman's Devotional	$10	
	B44	31 Secrets For Career Success	$10	
	B45	101 Wisdom Keys	$ 7	
	B46	31 Facts About Wisdom	$ 7	
	B47	The Covenant Of The Fifty-Eight Blessings	$ 8	
	B48	31 Keys To A New Beginning	$ 7	
	B49	The Proverbs 31 Woman	$ 7	
	B50	One-Minute Pocket Bible For The Achiever	$ 5	
	B51	One-Minute Pocket Bible For Fathers	$ 5	
	B52	One-Minute Pocket Bible For Mothers	$ 5	

Mail to: **Dr. Mike Murdock •The Wisdom Training Center • P.O. Box 99 • Denton, TX 76202**
(940) 891-1400 Or USA Call Toll Free 1-888-WISDOM-1

QTY	CODE	BOOK TITLE	USA	TOTAL
	B53	ONE-MINUTE POCKET BIBLE FOR TEENAGERS	$ 5	
	B54	ONE-MINUTE DEVOTIONAL (HARDBACK)	$14	
	B55	20 KEYS TO A HAPPIER MARRIAGE	$ 3	
	B56	HOW TO TURN MISTAKES INTO MIRACLES	$ 3	
	B57	31 SECRETS OF THE UNFORGETTABLE WOMAN	$ 9	
	B58	MENTOR'S MANNA ON ATTITUDE	$ 3	
	B59	THE MAKING OF A CHAMPION	$ 6	
	B60	ONE-MINUTE POCKET BIBLE FOR MEN	$ 5	
	B61	ONE-MINUTE POCKET BIBLE FOR WOMEN	$ 5	
	B62	ONE-MINUTE POCKET BIBLE/BUS.PROFESSIONALS	$ 5	
	B63	ONE-MINUTE POCKET BIBLE FOR TRUCKERS	$ 5	
	B64	7 OBSTACLES TO ABUNDANT SUCCESS	$ 3	
	B65	BORN TO TASTE THE GRAPES	$ 3	
	B66	GREED, GOLD AND GIVING	$ 3	
	B67	GIFT OF WISDOM FOR CHAMPIONS	$ 8	
	B68	GIFT OF WISDOM FOR ACHIEVERS	$ 8	
	B69	WISDOM KEYS FOR A POWERFUL PRAYER LIFE	$ 3	
	B70	GIFT OF WISDOM FOR MOTHERS	$ 8	
	B71	WISDOM - GOD'S GOLDEN KEY TO SUCCESS	$ 7	
	B72	THE GREATEST SUCCESS HABIT ON EARTH	$ 3	
	B73	THE MENTOR'S MANNA ON ABILITIES	$ 3	
	B74	THE ASSIGNMENT: DREAM/DESTINY #1	$10	
	B75	THE ASSIGNMENT: ANOINTING/ADVERSITY #2	$10	
	B76	THE MENTOR'S MANNA ON THE ASSIGNMENT	$ 3	
	B77	THE GIFT OF WISDOM FOR FATHERS	$ 8	
	B78	THE MENTOR'S MANNA ON THE SECRET PLACE	$ 3	
	B79	THE MENTOR'S MANNA ON ACHIEVEMENT	$ 3	
	B80	THE DOUBLE DIAMOND DAILY DEVOTIONAL	$12	
	B81	THE MENTOR'S MANNA ON ADVERSITY	$ 3	
	B82	31 REASONS PEOPLE DO NOT RECEIVE THEIR FINANCIAL HARVEST	$12	
	B83	THE GIFT OF WISDOM FOR WIVES	$ 8	
	B84	THE GIFT OF WISDOM FOR HUSBANDS	$ 8	
	B85	THE GIFT OF WISDOM FOR TEENAGERS	$ 8	
	B86	THE GIFT OF WISDOM FOR LEADERS	$ 8	
	B87	THE GIFT OF WISDOM FOR GRADUATES	$ 8	
	B88	THE GIFT OF WISDOM FOR BRIDES	$ 8	
	B89	THE GIFT OF WISDOM FOR GROOMS	$ 8	
	B90	THE GIFT OF WISDOM FOR MINISTERS	$ 8	
	B91H	THE LEADERSHIP SECRETS OF JESUS (HDBK)	$15	
	B92	SECRETS OF THE JOURNEY (VOL. 1)	$ 5	
	B93	SECRETS OF THE JOURNEY (VOL. 2)	$ 5	
	B94	SECRETS OF THE JOURNEY (VOL. 3)	$ 5	
	B95	SECRETS OF THE JOURNEY (VOL. 4)	$ 5	

MIKE MURDOCK

- Began full-time evangelism at the age of 19, which has continued for 34 years.

- Has traveled and spoken to more than 14,000 audiences in 36 countries, including East Africa, the Orient, and Europe.

- Noted author of 115 books, including best sellers, *Wisdom for Winning, Dream Seeds and The Double Diamond Principle.*

- Created the popular *"Wisdom Topical Bible"* series for Businessmen, Mothers, Fathers, Teenagers, and the *One-Minute Pocket Bible.*

- Has composed more than 5,600 songs such as *I Am Blessed, You Can Make It, and Jesus Just The Mention Of Your Name,* recorded by many artists.

- Is the Founder of the Wisdom Center in Dallas, Texas.

- Has a weekly television program called *"Wisdom Keys With Mike Murdock".*

- He has appeared often on TBN, CBN, Oral Roberts and other television network programs.

- Is a Founding Trustee on the Board of International Charismatic Bible Ministries founded by Oral Roberts.

- Has seen over 3,400 accept the call into full-time ministry under his ministry.

- Has embraced his Assignment: *Pursuing... Possessing... And Publishing The Wisdom Of God To Heal The Broken In This Generation.*

THE MINISTRY

1 **Wisdom Books & Literature** -115 best-selling Wisdom books and Teaching tapes that teach the Wisdom of God to thousands.

2 **Church Crusades** - Multitudes are ministered to in crusades and seminars throughout America in "The Uncommon Wisdom Conferences."

3 **Music Ministry** - Millions have been blessed by the anointed songwriting and singing of Mike Murdock, who has written over 5,600 songs.

4 **Television** - "Wisdom Keys With Mike Murdock," a nationally-syndicated weekly television program.

5 **The Wisdom Center** - Where Dr. Murdock holds annual Schools of Ministry for those training for a more excellent ministry.

6 **Schools of the Holy Spirit** - Mike Murdock hosts Schools of the Holy Spirit to mentor believers on the Person and companionship of the Holy Spirit.

7 **Schools of Wisdom** - Each year Mike Murdock hosts Schools of Wisdom for those who want personalized and advanced training for achieving "The Uncommon Dream."

8 **Missionary Ministry** - Dr. Murdock's overseas outreaches to 36 countries have included crusades to East Africa, South America, and Europe.

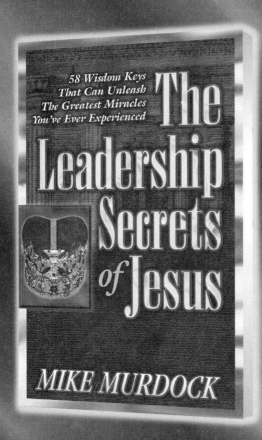

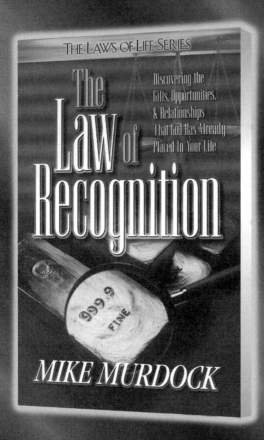

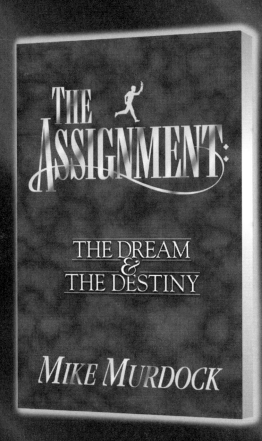

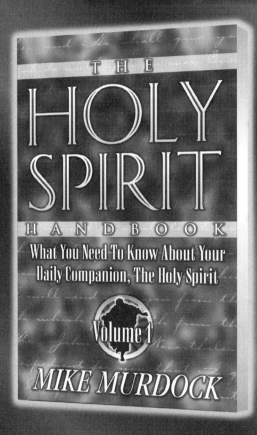

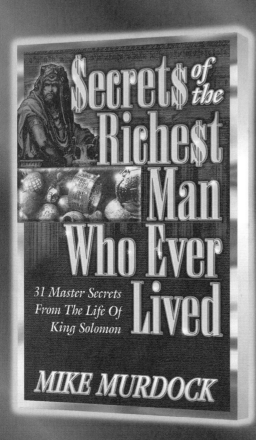

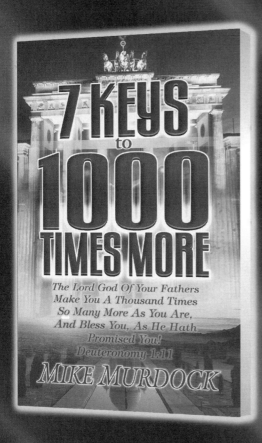

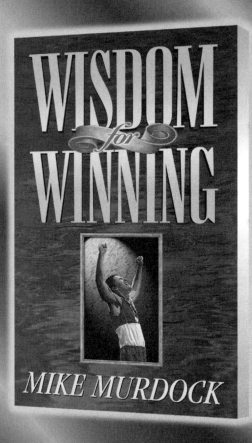

Run To Win.

- ▶ 10 Ingredients For Success...p.31
- ▶ Ten Lies Many People Believe About Money...p. 67
- ▶ 20 Keys For Winning At Work...p. 96
- ▶ 20 Keys To A Better Marriage...p. 101
- ▶ 3 Facts Every Parent Should Remember...p.106
- ▶ 5 Steps Out Of Depression...p. 121
- ▶ The Greatest Wisdom Principle I Ever Learned...p.167
- ▶ 7 Keys To Answered Prayer...p. 176
- ▶ God's Master Golden Key To Total Success...p. 183
- ▶ The Key To Understanding Life...p. 196

and much more!

Everyone needs to feel they have achieved something with their life. When we stop producing, loneliness and laziness will choke all enthusiasm from our living. What would you like to be doing? What are you doing about it? Get started on a project in your life. Start building on your dreams. Resist those who would control and change your personal goals. Get going with this powerful teaching and reach your life goals!

Wisdom Is The Principal Thing
Wisdom Is The Principal Thing
B-01
$10.00

Available also on six tapes for only $30!

The Wisdom Center – P.O. Box 99 – Denton, Texas – 76202
940-891-1400 – Fax: 940-891-4500 – www.mikemurdock.com